Lorena Garcia's

NEW
TACO
CLASSICS

Lorena Garcia's
NEW
TACO
CLASSICS

Lorena Garcia

with Liz Balmaseda

A CELEBRA BOOK

Celebra
Published by the Penguin Group
Penguin Group (USA) LLC, 375 Hudson Street,
New York, New York 10014

USA | Canada | UK | Ireland | Australia | New Zealand | India | South Africa |
China
penguin.com
A Penguin Random House Company

First published by Celebra,
a division of Penguin Group (USA) LLC

First Printing, October 2015

LIBRARY OF CONGRESS CATALOGING-IN-PUBLICATION DATA

GARCIA, LORENA (CHEF)
Lorena Garcia's new taco classics / Lorena Garcia.
    PAGES CM
  ISBN 978-0-451-47691-3
  1. Tacos. I. Title. II. Title: New taco classics.
TX836.G37 2015
641.84—DC23   2015008294

10 9 8 7 6 5 4 3 2 1

Set in Archer, Gotham, Twentieth Century MT
Designed by Pauline Neuwirth

I dedicate this book to the entire team that made this book a reality. To my mother, who gave me the vision to view life in the best possible way. As well as all of the Latin Americans who have come to this country, fallen in love, and are proud to be called Americans.

CONTENTS

CHAPTER 4: PICOS 64

CHAPTER 5: PICKLED RECIPES 95

CHAPTER 6: CREMAS 101

CHAPTER 7: SLAWS   111

NEW TACO CLASSICS

THE FILLINGS

CHAPTER 8: CHICKEN & POULTRY   135

CHAPTER 9: PORK   166

NEW TACO CLASSICS
THE SIDES

CHAPTER 13: SIDES   299

Chicken Churrasco Tacos,
see recipe on page 155

The New Taco Template

Like its people, the street foods of Latin America welcome you with a warm hug. Our stories may be different, our intonations unique, our rhythms purely regional, but one way or another our most beloved dishes come cradled in corn.

These dishes offer bites within bites, sublime pops of flavor contained within earthy corn wrappings. As simple as a taco, an arepa or a tamal may seem, they enfold more than a set of ingredients. They carry the great intangibles that distinguish our stories, the flavor notes of a particular city, the cooking methods of a region, not to mention the shared memories of a family.

Like tiny declarations of identity, each bite spells out the nuances between Mexico and Venezuela, Ecuador and Puerto Rico, Peru and Cuba.

Dishes tell stories. Sometimes those stories echo the beats of a particular place or culture, and sometimes they echo a mix of beats.

And when we explore the culinary beats we share in Latin America and the Caribbean, we must pay homage to the taco.

Allow me to use this term loosely here. I'm not referring to the literal taco shell and taco filling that may come to mind, but rather a concept that's shared across our Latin cultures: the concept of food in a vessel. Food embraced.

So what if we take that vessel as a way to showcase the broader Latin cuisine? What if we were to expand the concept of the humble taco and build a new taco template?

We build this template by first deconstructing the concept: There is the vessel that's most often made of corn masa, the filling, the toppings and the techniques that bring those elements together.

That vessel can take the form of a taco, an arepa, a sope, an empanada, even a tamal. It can carry any number of fillings and toppings,

and be paired with any number of sides. Master the elements and your mix-and-match possibilities are endless.

I see this book as a wonderful interactive meal in which you can bring your own pairing options to the table. I present you with scores of recipes, but you can combine them any way you'd like. And even though it's a taco book, you can skip the tortilla (or whatever vessel is specified in the recipe) entirely. That's the beauty of these recipes: They're made for pairing and sharing, depending on your craving or occasion.

You may notice, however, that these *New Taco Classics* recipes have a recurring theme in how they are constructed. For the most part, they are built in layers: vessel, filling, crunch and sauce.

- ✤ Your vessel can be crispy like a hard-shell taco or soft like a tamal.
- ✤ Your fillings—meats, seafood and/or veggies—give you the flavor centerpiece of your dish.
- ✤ Then there's the crunchy aspect: the slaws and salads that add textural contrast to the dish.
- ✤ Add a creamy or saucy element to help connect the flavors and you've got a deliciously complex bite.

The key to success is in developing layers of flavor that complement one another. It's all about balance and contrast.

It's also about freshness. I'm often reminded of the stellar fish tacos I've had in Playa del Carmen, Mexico. These are simple tacos made with simple ingredients by street food cooks. But the quality of ingredients elevates them to greatness. The fish is fresh-caught, the tortillas fresh-made, the toppings a study of contrasts—as in battered fish brightened by lime and cilantro notes dancing on fresh, creamy avocado. This is a bite that tells the story of its seaside city.

In my native Venezuela, the stories echo from little food carts that dot the streets. These are not like the hip food trucks that roam Los Angeles or Miami, but mobile stoves that turn out hot, fresh corn cakes stuffed with meats, cheese, beans, whatever your choice of filling may be.

What remains constant in these arepas is the undeniable essence of corn. Corn, from the sweet elote to the more rigid maiz, is the sturdy common thread that runs through the nuances of our cultures. It's an ingredient beloved throughout Latin America. But the type of corn that we choose, the way we cook it and the way we eat it—these change from culture to culture.

In my Venezuela, corn flour was one of the first ingredients I reached for as a child experimenting in my mother's kitchen. The aroma of masa harina wafting up from a hot comal, a searing griddle or a steaming pot of tamales still sends me back to one Caracas morning many years ago when I made my very first attempt at cooking. I was six years old and determined to make tamales for my mother and brother.

I slipped into the kitchen, scooped up some of my mother's precooked corn flour and mixed it into a masa paste, just as I had watched her do so many times. I spooned my tamale batter into ragged pieces of aluminum foil and dropped the foil packets into boiling water. Then I made some scrambled eggs to serve with these little tamalitos. Desayuno!

I set a small table in the middle of the living room and invited my mother and brother to come for breakfast. (My poor mother— what a mess I left in her kitchen!)

Still today, if you ask me to describe my favorite breakfast, I'd have to answer like a born and raised Venezuelan: arepas and eggs.

Breakfast is not breakfast in my homeland without a thick corn arepa, one that is so fluffy it can be split with a fork and filled. Fresh and ever so lightly sweet, it's our bread. Arepas in Venezuela are like morning biscuits in the American South.

In neighboring Colombia, the arepa is a bit thinner, but still flavorful and equally revered.

Travel the Andean highlands from Chile to Ecuador and find hearty wedges of pastel de choclo.

In Brazil, corn flour lends earthy goodness to the bolo de fubá corn cake that's so loved with morning coffee.

Travel north to Central America and you'll find a range of hand-patted tortillas, thick, thin and filled. In Nicaragua and Honduras, tortillas tend to be thinner and more pliable, perfect for wrapping grilled meats in. Salvadorans, who like their tortillas smaller and thicker, nosh on hearty pupusas, thick corn tortillas stuffed with everything from ground chorizo to chicharrón.

In Mexico, masa handling is more than an art—it's a culinary science. The hard maíz dough, made more pliable, healthful and

flavorful by an ancient alkalizing process known as nixtamalization, takes on a staggering number of forms: tacos, sopes, huaraches, tostadas, and others.

In Cuba, cornmeal that's studded with pork and aromatics is wrapped into a corn husk and simmered in water to make tamales.

So, how did we go from tacos to tamales? Trace the route from masa to filling to topping and you may be surprised at just how many "taco template" dishes you'll find.

As chefs, our art is the food we explore, cook and serve. This is how we connect with the world and why we always want to "say" something with our dishes. For me there is nothing better than to create a meal with my hands—a meal that comes from my heart—and feed others.

While I take inspiration from classic renditions of favorite Latin American dishes, I make them my own by experimenting with savory and sweet notes, with contrasting elements, with flavors that brazenly cross culinary and geographical borders. I encourage you to do the same. This is what *New Taco Classics* is all about.

We'll get creative with our ingredients. We'll use herbs and veggies and beans to flavor the corn masa. We'll reach for plantain leaves instead of aluminum foil to wrap our tamales. We'll experiment with a variety of slaws and salsas and cremas.

That is my aim in writing this book—to honor our shared cuisine in dishes that are fresh, modern and thoroughly Latin.

These recipes, for the most part, do not require hours of labor at the stove. They are meant to be accessible, shareable and celebration-worthy, even on a weeknight.

Some of these taco variations enclose their contents entirely, others offer a small peek, and others greet you with an open face. But one way or another, this much is true: They all welcome you with a warm hug and an open heart.

—Lorena Garcia

THE BASE

CHAPTER 1

MASA / DOUGH

ALL HAIL QUEEN CORN.

Corn dough, flavorful and resilient, offers the perfect vessel for our fillings, from saucy or grilled meats to melted cheeses to marinated seafood or crispy fried fish to slow, beautiful braises.

As simple as a taco or arepa shell may seem, there's nothing plain about its corn foundation. With its nutty, almost mineral scents corn lends an earthy subplot to the main story lines of Latin American cuisine.

But imagine adding flavor notes to the masa—the dough—that echo or contrast a taco's filling. We'll do this by infusing the dough for Venezuelan telitas—flat breads—with beets for a dramatically hued result, and with cilantro for a fresh, herbaceous finish.

We'll add pops of flavor and color to tamales with roasted red peppers and brilliantly colored achiote oil. And we'll deepen the flavors of classic reinitas with fresh carrots and black beans.

Those keeping a gluten-free diet are in for a treat: The majority of the recipes in this chapter are wheat-free and offer delicious alternatives to your average gluten-free flour mixes. Of course, because corn masa is gluten-free, it requires some love and finesse to keep it from crumbling.

A word about prep work: If you don't have time to make your own corn vessel, you can substitute store-bought tortillas. But I hope the following recipes will encourage you to try the homemade approach. With a little practice, you'll find that working with corn masa is not as daunting as you may think.

RECIES

PREP TIME: 20 minutes

COOK TIME: 15 minutes

YIELD: 8 (4½ ounces each)

AREPAS

These fluffy disks are ever-present in Venezuelan and Colombian cuisine. Easily made with precooked corn flour, arepas are as adaptable as they are delicious—enjoy them at breakfast, lunch, dinner, or snack time.

1. In a mixing bowl, combine the precooked corn flour and salt. Add the water and knead the mixture until all the ingredients are well combined and the dough no longer sticks to your hands. (If, while kneading, the dough seems too stiff and breaks apart, add a few tablespoons of hot water; if it is too sticky, add a little more corn flour).

2. Divide the dough into 8 equal balls (about 4½ ounces each) and flatten each between your palms into a 4-inch patty, ½-inch thick.

3. Heat the vegetable oil in a large nonstick skillet over medium-low heat for 2 minutes. Add 3 or 4 arepas to the pan (depending on size of pan). The arepas should sizzle as they hit the skillet.

4. Cook the arepas until they're golden and have a nice crust, 6 to 8 minutes. Flip them and brown the other side for an additional 6 to 8 minutes. Then cover the arepas and continue to steam them for another 5 minutes.

INGREDIENTS:

2 cups precooked corn flour (masa arepa flour)

1 tablespoon kosher salt

2½ cups water

1 tablespoon vegetable oil (for greasing skillet)

TELITAS (FLAT BREADS)

The word "telita," which means "little cloth" or a tiny scrap of cloth, inspired these thin, corn-scented flat breads. Made with precooked corn flour, they can be enjoyed soft or fried crispy. Either way, they welcome flavor experimentation. Infuse them with cheese or black beans for a richer flavor, with beets or carrots for a pop of color, with cilantro for a herbaceous note, or with anise seed and panela or piloncillo for a sweet finish.

PREP TIME: 15 minutes

COOK TIME: 5–6 minutes

YIELD: 12 rounds (1½ ounces each)

CHEESE TELITAS

1. Whisk together the corn flour and salt.
2. In a medium-size bowl, add the water, queso fresco cheese, and oil. Slowly add the flour mixture, stirring until well combined. The dough will be loose at first, but the flour will absorb the liquid.
3. Start to knead the dough in the bowl, and once it becomes very soft and does not stick to your hands, after about 5 minutes, the dough is ready to be shaped. (If while kneading, the dough seems too stiff and breaks apart, add a few tablespoons of water; if it is too sticky, add a little more flour.)
4. Divide the dough into 12 equal balls, of 1½ ounces each, and flatten each in a tortilla press or by using the flat side of a plate to make 5-inch tortillas.

FRIED METHOD:

1. Preheat the fryer to 350F degrees. Fry the telitas, 3 to 4 at a time, until golden brown, about 2½ minutes per side.
2. Place the fried telitas in a plate lined with paper towels until ready to use.

ASADA METHOD STOVE TOP/SKILLET:

1. Heat a large skillet or griddle over medium-high heat. Place telitas in the hot pan. Cook the telita until it is browned and crispy, 2 to 3 minutes. Flip it over and brown the other side, 2 to 3 minutes longer.
2. Remove from pan and set aside in a tortilla warmer or wrapped in a kitchen towel.

INGREDIENTS:

1 cup precooked corn flour (masa arepa flour)

1 teaspoon kosher salt

1 cup water

¾ cup queso fresco cheese, grated

1 tablespoon vegetable oil

PREP TIME: 20 minutes

COOK TIME: 6 minutes

YIELD: 12 rounds (1-ounce each)

ANISE-AND-PILONCILLO TELITAS

INGREDIENTS:

1 cup water

3 tablespoons panela (unrefined cane sugar), grated

1 tablespoon anise seed

1 cup precooked corn flour (masa arepa flour)

2 tablespoons all-purpose flour

¾ cups queso blanco, grated

1 tablespoon butter

1 teaspoon kosher salt

1. In a pot, add water, panela, and anise seed and cook over medium heat for 5 minutes. Let rest 15 minutes until warm to the touch.
2. In a mixing bowl add the panela-and-anise water. Add the remaining ingredients and combine. Mix well with hands until all the ingredients are incorporated and the dough does not stick to your hands.
3. Divide the dough into 12 equal balls, 1-ounce each, and flatten in a tortilla press, pressing about ¾ of the way down to make 4-inch rounds that are about ¼-inch thick.
4. Heat a large skillet, plancha, or griddle over medium-high heat. Place telitas in hot pan. Cook the telita until it is browned and crispy, 3 minutes. Flip it over and brown the other side, 2 to 3 minutes longer.
5. Remove from pan and place in a tortilla warmer or wrapped in a kitchen towel.

FRIED METHOD:

1. Follow telita recipe instructions through Step 4.
2. Fill a fryer with oil halfway up the pan. Heat oil to 350F degrees. Fry each telita for 2½ minutes on each side.
3. Remove and place on paper towels to drain. Serve immediately.

ASADA METHOD STOVE TOP/SKILLET:

1. Heat a large skillet or griddle over medium-high heat. Place telitas in the hot pan. Cook the telita until it is browned and crispy, 2 to 3 minutes. Flip it over and brown the other side, 2 to 3 minutes longer.
2. Remove from pan and set aside in a tortilla warmer or wrapped in a kitchen towel.

PREP TIME: 20 minutes

COOK TIME: 5–6 minutes

YIELD: 12 rounds (1-ounce each)

BEET TELITAS

1. In a blender, place beets, water, oil, and salt. Blend until ingredients are well combined, about 30 seconds.
2. In a medium-size bowl, add the beet mixture and slowly add to it the corn flour, stirring until well combined. The dough will be loose at first, but the flour will absorb the liquid.
3. Start to knead the dough in the bowl, and once it becomes very soft and does not stick to your hands, after about 5 minutes, the dough is ready to be shaped. (If while kneading, the dough seems too stiff and breaks apart, add a few tablespoons of water; if it's too sticky, add a little more flour.)
4. Divide the dough into 12 equal balls, 1½-ounces each, and flatten in a tortilla press (or by using the back of a flat plate), pressing about ¾ of the way down to make 4-inch rounds that are about ¼-inch thick.
5. Heat a large skillet or griddle over medium-high heat. Place telitas in a hot pan. Cook each telita until it is browned and crispy, 2 to 3 minutes. Flip it over and brown the other side, 2 to 3 minutes longer.
6. Remove from pan and place in a tortilla warmer or wrapped in a kitchen towel.

INGREDIENTS:

¾ cup canned beets, strained

1 cup water

1 tablespoon vegetable oil

1 teaspoon kosher salt

1 cup precooked corn flour (masa arepa flour)

FRIED METHOD:

1. Follow telita recipe instructions through Step 4.
2. Fill a fryer with oil halfway up the pan. Heat oil to 350F degrees. Fry each telita for 2½ minutes on each side.
3. Remove and place on paper towels to drain. Serve immediately.

ASADA METHOD STOVE TOP/SKILLET:

1. Heat a large skillet or griddle over medium-high heat. Place telitas in the hot pan. Cook the telita until it is browned and crispy, 2 to 3 minutes. Flip it over and brown the other side, 2 to 3 minutes longer.
2. Remove from pan and set aside in a tortilla warmer or wrapped in a kitchen towel.

PREP TIME: 15 minutes

COOK TIME: 5–6 minutes

YIELD: 12 rounds (1½ ounces each)

CILANTRO TELITAS

INGREDIENTS:

1 cup precooked corn flour (masa arepa flour)

1 teaspoon kosher salt

1 cup water

¾ cup fresh cilantro, with stems

1 tablespoon vegetable oil

1. Whisk together the corn flour and salt.
2. Place water and cilantro in a blender. Mix until water and cilantro are well combined, about 30 seconds.
3. In a medium-size bowl, add the water-and-cilantro mixture and oil. Slowly add the flour mixture, stirring until well combined. The dough will be loose at first, but the flour will absorb the liquid.
4. Start to knead the dough in the bowl, and once it becomes very soft and does not stick to your hands, after about 5 minutes, the dough is ready to be shaped. (If while kneading, the dough seems too stiff and breaks apart, add a few tablespoons of water; if it is too sticky, add a little more flour.)
5. Divide the dough into 12 equal balls, 1½ ounces each, and flatten each in a tortilla press or by using the flat side of a plate to make 5-inch tortillas.

FRIED METHOD:

1. Preheat the fryer to 350F degrees. Fry the telitas, 3 to 4 at a time, until golden brown, about 2½ minutes per side.
2. Place the fried telitas in a plate lined with paper towels until ready to use.

ASADA METHOD STOVE TOP/SKILLET:

1. Heat a large skillet or griddle over medium-high heat. Place telitas in the hot pan. Cook the telita until it is browned and crispy, 2 to 3 minutes. Flip it over and brown the other side, 2 to 3 minutes longer.
2. Remove from pan and set aside in a tortilla warmer or wrapped in a kitchen towel.

PREP TIME: 20 minutes

COOK TIME: 5–6 minutes

YIELD: 12 rounds (1½ ounces each)

CARROT TELITAS

1. Whisk together the flour and salt.
2. Place water and carrot in a blender. Mix until water and carrots are well combined, about 30 seconds.
3. In a medium-size bowl, add the water-and-carrot mixture and oil, then slowly add the flour mixture, stirring until well combined. The dough will be loose at first, but will thicken as the flour absorbs the liquid.
4. Start to knead the dough in the bowl, and once it becomes very soft and does not stick to your hands, after about 5 minutes, the dough is ready to be shaped. (If while kneading, the dough seems too stiff and breaks apart, add a few table-spoons of water; if it is too sticky, add a little more flour.)
5. Divide the dough into 12 equal balls, 1½ ounces each, and flatten in a tortilla press (or by using the back of a flat plate), pressing about ¾ of the way down to make 4-inch rounds that are about ¼-inch thick.
6. Heat a large lightly oiled skillet, plancha, or griddle over medium-high heat. Place telitas in hot pan. Cook the telita until it is browned and crispy, 3 minutes. Flip it over and brown the other side, 3 minutes longer.
7. Remove from pan and place in a tortilla warmer or wrapped in a kitchen towel.

FRIED METHOD:

1. Follow telita recipe instructions through Step 4.
2. Fill a fryer with oil halfway up the pan. Heat oil to 350F de-grees. Fry each telita for 2½ minutes on each side.
3. Remove and place on paper towels to drain. Serve immediately.

ASADA METHOD STOVE TOP/SKILLET:

1. Heat a large skillet or griddle over medium-high heat. Place telitas in the hot pan. Cook the telita until it is browned and crispy, 2 to 3 minutes. Flip it over and brown the other side, 2 to 3 minutes longer.
2. Remove from pan and set aside in a tortilla warmer or wrapped in a kitchen towel.

INGREDIENTS:

1 cup precooked corn flour (masa arepa flour)

1 teaspoon kosher salt

1 cup water

¾ cup carrots, grated

1 tablespoon vegetable oil

PREP TIME: 20 minutes

COOK TIME: 5–6 minutes

YIELD: 12 rounds (1½ ounce each)

INGREDIENTS:

¾ cup, black beans (cooked)

½ cup water

1 tablespoon vegetable oil

1 teaspoon kosher salt

1 cup precooked corn flour (masa arepa flour)

2 tablespoons all-purpose flour

BLACK BEAN TELITAS

1. In a blender, place black beans, water, oil, and salt. Blend until ingredients are well combined, about 30 seconds.
2. In a medium-size bowl, add the black bean mixture and slowly add the corn flour and the all-purpose flour, stirring until well combined. The dough will be loose at first, but the flour will absorb the liquid.
3. Start to knead the dough in the bowl, and once it becomes very soft and does not stick to your hands, after about 5 minutes, the dough is ready to be shaped. (If while kneading, the dough seems too stiff and breaks apart, add a few tablespoons of water; if it is too sticky, add a little more flour.)
4. Divide the dough into 12 equal balls, 1½ ounces each, and flatten them in a tortilla press, pressing about ¾ of the way down to make 4-inch rounds that are about ¼ inch thick.

FRIED METHOD:

In a fryer with oil at 350F degrees, fry each telita for 2½ minutes per side. Remove and place on paper towels to drain. Serve immediately.

ASADA METHOD STOVE TOP/SKILLET:

1. Heat a large skillet or griddle over medium-high heat. Place telitas in the hot pan. Cook the telita until it is browned and crispy, 2 to 3 minutes. Flip it over and brown the other side, 2 to 3 minutes longer.
2. Remove from pan and set aside in a tortilla warmer or wrapped in a kitchen towel.

PURPLE (PERUVIAN) CORN TELITAS

1. Boil corn in water for at least 3 hours until tender. Corn and water will reduce to about 2½ cups. Place cooled water and corn in blender, add oil, and blend until completely smooth.
2. Place blended purple corn into a large bowl. Add salt, precooked cornmeal, and self-rising flour.
3. Start to knead the dough in the bowl, and once it becomes very soft and does not stick to your hands, after about 10 minutes, the dough is ready to be shaped. (If the dough stiffens or breaks apart while you are kneading it, add a few tablespoons of water. If it is too sticky, add a little more flour.)
4. Divide the dough into 12 equal balls, 1½ ounces each, and flatten in a tortilla press (or by using the back of a flat plate), about ¾ of the way down, into 4-inch rounds about ¼-inch thick.

FRIED METHOD:

In a fryer with oil at 350F degrees, fry each telita for 2½ minutes per side. Remove and place on paper towels to drain. Serve immediately.

ASADA METHOD STOVE TOP/SKILLET:

Heat a large skillet, plancha or griddle over medium-high heat. Place telitas in the hot pan. Cook the disk until it is browned and crispy, 2 to 3 minutes. Flip it over and brown the other side, 2 to 3 minutes longer. Remove from pan and place in a tortilla holder or wrap them in a kitchen towel.

PREP TIME: 10 minutes

COOK TIME: 3 hours, 20 minutes

TOTAL TIME: 3 hours, 30 minutes

YIELDS: 8

INGREDIENTS:

4 purple corn cobs

1 gallon plus 1 quart water

3 tablespoons vegetable oil

1½ tablespoons kosher salt

1¾ cup precooked cornmeal

¼ cup self-rising flour

REINITAS

As her royal name suggests, a reinita (little queen) demands her crown. These small, crispy arepas are the perfect two-bite snack. Top them or fill them with anything from tuna salad to fresh ceviche to a pinch of hot pulled pork. The crowning touch can be as simple or as dramatic as you'd like. And as with the telitas, the reinita masa can be infused with herbs or veggies for added flavor and color.

PREP TIME: 20 minutes

COOK TIME: 5–6 minutes

YIELD: 12 patties (1 ounce each)

CLASSIC REINITAS

1. Whisk together the flour and salt.
2. In a medium-size bowl, add the water and oil. Slowly add the flour mixture, stirring until well combined. The dough will be loose at first, but will thicken as the flour absorbs the liquid.
3. Start to knead the dough in the bowl, and once it becomes very soft and does not stick to your hands, after about 5 minutes, the dough is ready to be shaped. (If while kneading, the dough seems too stiff and breaks apart, add a few tablespoons of water; if it is too sticky, add a little more flour.)
4. Divide the dough into 12 equal balls, 1 ounce each, and flatten each between your palms into 2½-inch patties that are about ½-inch thick.
5. Preheat the fryer to 350F degrees.
6. Fry the reinitas, 3 to 4 at a time, until golden brown, about 2½ minutes per side.
7. Place the fried reinitas on a plate lined with paper towels until ready to use.

INGREDIENTS:

1 cup precooked corn flour (masa arepa flour)

1 teaspoon kosher salt

1 cup water

1 tablespoon vegetable oil

PREP TIME: 20 minutes

COOK TIME: 5–6 minutes

YIELD: 12 patties (1 ounce each)

INGREDIENTS:

1 cup precooked corn flour (masa arepa flour)

1 teaspoon kosher salt

1 cup water

¾ cup canned beets, drained

1 tablespoon vegetable oil

BEET REINITAS

1. Whisk together the flour and salt.
2. Place water and beets in a blender. Mix until well combined, about 30 seconds.
3. In a medium-size bowl, add the beet mixture and oil. Slowly add the flour mixture, stirring until well combined. The dough will be loose at first, but will firm up as the liquid is absorbed into the flour.
4. Start to knead the dough in the bowl, and once it becomes very soft and does not stick to your hands, after about 5 minutes, the dough is ready to be shaped. (If while kneading, the dough seems too stiff and breaks apart, add a few tablespoons of water; if it is too sticky, add a little more flour.)
5. Divide the dough into 12 equal balls, 1 ounce each, and flatten them between your palms into 2½-inch patties that are about ½-inch thick.
6. Preheat the fryer to 350F degrees.
7. Fry the reinitas, 3 to 4 at a time, until golden brown, about 2½ minutes per side.
8. Place the fried reinitas on a plate lined with paper towels until ready to use.

PREP TIME: 20 minutes

COOK TIME: 5–6 minutes

YIELD: 15 patties (1 ounce each)

CILANTRO REINITAS

1. Whisk together the flour and salt.
2. Place water and cilantro in a blender. Mix until well combined, about 30 seconds.
3. In a medium-size bowl, add the cilantro mixture and oil. Slowly add the flour mixture, stirring until well combined. The dough will be loose at first, but will thicken as the flour absorbs the liquid.
4. Start to knead the dough in the bowl and once it becomes very soft and does not stick to your hands, after about 5 minutes, the dough is ready to be shaped. (If while kneading, the dough seems too stiff and breaks apart, add a few tablespoons of water; if it is too sticky, add a little more flour.)
5. Divide the dough into 15 equal balls, 1 ounce each, and flatten each between your palms into a 2½-inch patty that's about ½-inch thick.
6. Preheat the fryer at 350F degrees.
7. Fry the reinitas, 3 to 4 at a time, until golden brown, about 2½ minutes per side.
8. Place the fried reinitas on a plate lined with paper towels until ready to use.

INGREDIENTS:

1 cup precooked corn flour (masa arepa flour)

1 teaspoon kosher salt

1 cup water

¾ cup fresh cilantro, with stems

1 tablespoon vegetable oil

PREP TIME: 20 minutes

COOK TIME: 5–6 minutes

YIELD: 12 patties (1 ounce each)

CARROT REINITAS

INGREDIENTS:

1 cup precooked corn flour (masa arepa flour)

1 teaspoon kosher salt

1 cup water

¾ cup carrots, grated

1 tablespoon vegetable oil

1. Whisk together the flour and salt.
2. Place water and carrot in a blender. Mix until water and carrots are well combined, about 30 seconds.
3. In a medium-size bowl, add the carrot mixture and oil. Slowly add the flour mixture, stirring until well combined. The dough will be loose at first, but will thicken as the flour absorbs the liquid.
4. Start to knead the dough in the bowl, and once it becomes very soft and does not stick to your hands, after about 5 minutes, the dough is ready to be shaped. (If while kneading, the dough seems too stiff and breaks apart, add a few tablespoons of water; if it is too sticky, add a little more flour.)
5. Divide the dough into 12 equal balls, 1 ounce each, and flatten each between your palms into a 2½-inch patty that is about ½-inch thick.
6. Preheat the fryer at 350F degrees.
7. Fry the reinitas, 3 to 4 at a time, until golden brown, about 2½ minutes per side.

PREP TIME: 20 minutes

COOK TIME: 5–6 minutes

YIELD: 12 patties (1 ounce each)

BLACK BEAN REINITAS

1. Whisk together the flour and salt.
2. Place water and black beans in a blender. Mix until well combined, about 30 seconds.
3. In a medium-size bowl, add the black bean mixture and oil. Slowly add the flour mixture, stirring until well combined. The dough will be loose at first, but the flour will absorb the liquid.
4. Start to knead the dough in the bowl, and once it becomes very soft and does not stick to your hands, after about 5 minutes, the dough is ready to be shaped. (If while kneading, the dough seems too stiff and breaks apart, add a few tablespoons of water; if it is too sticky, add a little more flour.)
5. Divide the dough into 12 equal balls, 1 ounce each, and flatten each between your palms into a 2½-inch patty that's about ½-inch thick.
6. Preheat the fryer at 350F degrees.
7. Fry the reinitas, 3 to 4 at a time, until golden brown, about 2½ minutes per side.
8. Place the fried reinitas on a plate lined with paper towels until ready to use.

INGREDIENTS:

1 cup precooked corn flour (masa arepa flour)

1 teaspoon kosher salt

1 cup water

¾ cup canned black beans, strained

1 tablespoon vegetable oil

TORTILLAS AND TOSTADAS

A fresh tortilla is the cornerstone of a classic taco, simplicity in a thin, earthy disk. A soft tortilla not only enfolds its contents, but also helps in sopping up the filling's juices. A crispy tortilla lends wonderful contrast to a taco's fillings. As for a freshly fried tostada: Consider it a deliciously crispy base for any amount or combo of toppings. It offers your dish an underlying element of crunch.

PREP TIME: 25 minutes

COOK TIME: 8 minutes

YIELD: 12 tortillas
(1-ounce, 4-inch rounds)

SOFT CORN TORTILLAS

1. Whisk together oil, salt, and water in a large bowl. Set aside.
2. Whisk together the corn flour and baking powder. Add flour mixture to the liquid mixture, stirring until well combined. The dough will be loose at first, but will firm up quickly as the flour absorbs the liquid.
3. Knead the dough until it becomes compact and no longer sticks to your hands. Cover the dough tightly with plastic wrap to prevent a skin from forming. After about 15 minutes, the dough is ready to be shaped.
4. Divide the dough into 12 equal balls, 1 ounce each, and flatten in tortilla press (or by using the back of a flat plate), pressing all the way down to make 4-inch rounds.
5. Heat a large skillet or griddle over medium-high heat. Working in batches, place tortillas in hot pan. Cook each tortilla until it is browned and crispy, about 4 minutes. Flip it over and brown the other side, 4 minutes longer.
6. Remove from pan and set aside in a tortilla warmer or wrapped in a kitchen towel. Use immediately or store in a zipped plastic bag in a refrigerator for up to a week.

INGREDIENTS:

1 tablespoon vegetable oil

¾ teaspoon kosher salt

1 cup water, room temperature

1 cup corn flour

2 tablespoons baking powder

HARD-SHELL TORTILLAS

HARD-SHELL METHOD:

1. In a skillet heat about 1 inch of oil over medium to medium-high heat 365F degrees.
2. Use tongs to place one tortilla at a time into the oil. It should start to sizzle right away. Fry for 15 seconds, then flip over and fold the shell in half, hold in place with tongs until crispy, about 15 seconds.

PREP TIME: 25 minutes

COOK TIME: 2 minutes

YIELD: 12 tostadas
(1-ounce, 4-inch rounds)

TOSTADAS

1. Follow tortilla instructions through Step 4.
2. To a frying pan, add about 1 inch of oil. Heat the oil on medium-high heat until it's sizzling hot, about 350F. (If the tortilla skin does not blister upon hitting the oil, the oil is not hot enough.)
3. One at a time, fry the tortillas until golden brown on both sides, about 45 seconds to 1 minute per side. (You can use metal tongs to push the tortilla under the hot oil, to turn, and to take out of the pan.) As you remove tortillas, allow the oil to drip off as much as possible before proceeding to the next step.
4. Place the tostadas in a paper-towel-lined tray to absorb the excess oil and, while hot, dust with a little kosher salt.

INGREDIENTS:

tortilla ingredients

vegetable oil, for frying

kosher salt, for finishing

PREP TIME: 25 minutes

COOK TIME: 6 minutes

YIELD: 12 tortillas
(1½-ounce, 5-inch rounds)

BLUE CORN TORTILLAS

INGREDIENTS:

1 cup of blue corn flour

1 cup of regular corn flour

1⅓ cup of water, room temperature

¼ teaspoon kosher salt

1 tablespoon butter, unsalted and room temperature

2 tablespoons vegetable oil, to grease the pan

1. In a mixing bowl, stir all the ingredients until well combined. The dough will be loose at first, but it will thicken as the flour mixture absorbs the liquid.
2. Start to knead the dough in the bowl, and once it becomes compact and doesn't stick to your hands, after about 5 minutes, the dough is ready. Let the dough sit for 15 minutes, covered with plastic wrap.
3. Divide the dough into 12 equal balls, 1½ ounces each, and flatten in tortilla press (or by using the back of a flat plate), pressing all the way down to make 5-inch rounds.
4. Heat a greased large skillet or griddle over medium-high heat. Place tortillas in hot pan. Cook the tortilla until it is browned and crispy (about 3 minutes). Flip it over and brown the other side, 3 minutes longer.
5. Remove from pan and place in a tortilla warmer or wrapped in a kitchen towel.

PREP TIME: 20 minutes

COOK TIME: 2–3 minutes

YIELD: 24 puffy tortillas

PUFFY TORTILLAS

A bit of all-purpose flour works like magic on these corn tortillas, allowing them to puff up. These pillow-like tortillas are delicious when topped with hearty Blood Sausage and Fava Bean Spread (page 255), Herb-Crusted Lamb Tenderloin (page 274), or simply Grilled Avocado (page 289).

INGREDIENTS:

2 tablespoons vegetable oil, plus oil for frying*

1½ teaspoon kosher salt

1½ cup water

2 cups corn flour

¼ cup all-purpose flour

2 tablespoons baking powder

1. Whisk together 2 tablespoons oil, salt, and water in a large bowl. Set aside.
2. Whisk together the corn flour, all-purpose flour, and baking powder. Add flour mixture to the liquid mixture, stirring until well combined. The dough will be loose at first, but will firm up as the flour absorbs the liquid.
3. Start to knead the dough in the bowl, and once it becomes compact and doesn't stick to your hands, after about 5 minutes, the dough is ready to be shaped.
4. Divide the dough into 24 equal balls, 1 ounce each, and flatten in tortilla press (or by using the back of a flat plate), pressing ¾ way down to make 4-inch rounds.
5. Heat a deep fryer with enough oil for deep frying to 350F. Place the puffy tortillas in hot oil until golden brown, about 1–2 minutes.
6. Remove from oil and place on paper towels to absorb excess oil.

---

* The amount of oil required for this recipe depends on the size of your pot or pan. Add enough oil to allow the puffy tortillas to swim around pan and fry more evenly.

INGREDIENTS:

1 tablespoon vegetable oil

¾ teaspoon kosher salt

1 cup water

1 cup corn flour

2 tablespoons baking powder

SOPES

With their distinctive crimped edges, these small, fried corn cakes provide an ideal vessel for braised meats or juicier fillings. The edges turn Mexico's beloved sopes into small, crispy bowls.

1. Whisk together oil, salt, and water in a large bowl. Set aside.

2. Whisk together the corn flour and baking powder. Add flour mixture to the liquid mixture, stirring until well combined. The dough will be loose at first, but the flour will absorb the liquid.

3. Start to knead the dough in the bowl, and once it becomes compact and no longer sticks to your hands, after about 5 minutes, the dough is ready to be shaped.

4. Divide the dough into 8 equal balls, 2 ounces each, and flatten in a tortilla press (or by using the back of a flat plate), pressing about ¾ of the way down to make 4-inch rounds that are about ¼-inch thick.

5. Heat a large skillet or griddle over medium-high heat. Place sopes in hot pan. Cook the sopes until browned and crispy, 3 minutes. Flip them over and brown the other side, 2 minutes longer.

6. Remove from pan. With your fingers, crimp 3 lines in the center of the sope. (This helps hold your sauce or filling in place.) Pinch dough upward around the edges to create a ½-inch rim.

7. Before serving, drop the sopes into a pan of hot vegetable oil (350F) for 3 seconds (a quick dip) and remove. This will crisp the sopes without overcooking them.

TAMALES

A good tamal is one of the great comfort dishes of Latin America. Enriched with masa and wrapped in corn husks, these soft and warm cylinders of goodness are steamed to a tender finish.

SWEET CORN TAMALES

1. Soak corn husks in hot water for about 30 minutes before assembling tamales.
2. In a large bowl, whisk together water, melted butter, milk, salt, and egg.
3. Stir in queso fresco, followed by the sweet corn flour.
4. In a food processor, place fresh corn and pulse for 10 seconds. Add corn to flour mixture, and combine well. Allow dough to rest for 5 minutes.

ASSEMBLE THE TAMALES:

1. Take 3 tablespoons (2 ounces) of corn mixture and place in the center of a softened corn husk.
2. Fold in sides of husk over filling, then fold in the top and bottom of the husk.
3. Create thin, long strips/string from one corn husk wrapper. Tie a corn husk string around the center of the tamale tightly. (You can use a rubber band instead of a corn husk string.)
4. Steam tamales (in a steamer basket of your choice) for 30 minutes.

INGREDIENTS:

1 package corn husk wrappers

1½ cups water

4 ounces of melted butter

¼ cup milk

2 teaspoons kosher salt

1 egg

¾ cup queso fresco

1⅓ cup precooked corn flour, masa arepa flour sweet corn flour (red package)

1 cup fresh yellow corn (kernels)

PREP TIME: 15 minutes

COOK TIME: 30 minutes

YIELD: 15 tamales

ROASTED RED PEPPER TAMALES

INGREDIENTS:

1 package corn husk wrappers

2 whole red bell peppers, roasted, seeded, and peeled*

1 cup water

1¼ tablespoons kosher salt

3 tablespoons butter, melted

2 cups precooked white corn flour

1. Soak corn husks in hot water for about 30 minutes before assembling tamales.
2. In a blender place roasted, seeded, and peeled red peppers, water, salt, and butter.
3. Place pepper mixture in a large bowl and add the white corn flour. Combine ingredients until they reach a smooth consistency.
4. Spread one softened corn husk on a flat surface. Take 3 tablespoons (2 ounces) of corn mixture and place in the center of husk.
5. Fold in sides of husk over filling, overlapping them, then fold in the top and bottom of the husk toward the center.
6. Create tamal ties by cutting one of the corn husk wrappers into long, thin strips. Tie one of the corn husk strips around the center of the tamal tightly, to secure. (You can use a rubber band instead of a corn husk string.)
7. Steam tamales (using a steamer basket of your choice) for 30 minutes.

* For two roasted red peppers, you'll need 1 tablespoon of vegetable oil. Roast the peppers, drizzled with the oil, on a foil-lined baking sheet in a 400-degree oven for 20 minutes. Flip the peppers and roast for another 20 minutes. Remove peppers and allow to cool, then remove the skin and seeds. You can also grill them over an open flame, rotating them every few minutes. In a pinch, you can use jarred roasted red peppers.

WHITE HOMINY CORN TORTILLAS, AREPAS, AND REINITAS

PREP TIME: 30 minutes

COOK TIME: 2 hours

YIELD: 12 tortillas (1 ounce each), 12 reinitas (1 ounce each), or 4 arepas (4 ounces each)

Hominy adds a texture and a touch of earthy elegance to tortillas and arepas. It requires soaking and grinding, but it's worth the effort to achieve delicious results.

INGREDIENTS:

12 cups water, to cook hominy corn

14 ounces white hominy corn, softened*

½ tablespoon kosher salt

1 cup grated queso fresco

2 tablespoons vegetable oil (add 1 tablespoon if making arepas)

PREP THE CORN:

1. Grind cooled corn utilizing smallest grinder attachment. Pass corn through grinder twice.
2. Combine corn with salt, cheese, and oil into dough until all ingredients have been well incorporated.

TO MAKE TORTILLAS: SEE "TORTILLAS AND TOSTADAS" SECTION (PAGE 22).

1. Divide the dough into 12 equal balls, 1 ounce each, and flatten in tortilla press (or by using the back of a flat plate), pressing all the way down to make 4-inch rounds.
2. Heat a large skillet or griddle over medium-high heat. Working in batches, place tortillas in hot pan. Cook each tortilla until it is browned and crispy, about 4 minutes. Flip it over and brown the other side, 4 minutes longer.
3. Remove from pan and set aside in a tortilla warmer or wrapped in a kitchen towel. Use immediately or store in a zipped plastic bag in a refrigerator for up to a week.

TO MAKE REINITAS:

1. Divide the dough into 12 equal balls, 1 ounce each, and flatten each between your palms into 2½-inch patties that are about ½-inch thick.
2. Preheat the fryer to 350F degrees.

---

* Soaking corn overnight will produce the best results. If not, place water and corn in a saucepan and cook on medium heat for two hours until softened. Drain the corn and reserve the liquid for another recipe. Set corn aside to cool off.

(recipe continues)

3. Fry the reinitas, 3 to 4 at a time, until golden brown, about 2½ minutes per side.
4. Place the fried reinitas on a plate lined with paper towels until ready to use.

TO MAKE AREPAS:
1. Divide the dough into 4 equal balls, about 4 ounces each, and flatten each between your palms to make a 4-inch patty that's ½-inch thick.
2. Heat 1 tablespoon of the oil in a large nonstick skillet over medium-low heat for 2 minutes. Add 3 or 4 arepas to the pan (depending on size of your pan). The arepas should sizzle as they hit the skillet.
3. Cook the arepas until they're golden and have a nice crust, 6 to 8 minutes. Flip them and brown the other side for an additional 6 to 8 minutes. Cover the arepas and continue to steam them for another 5 minutes.

CHAPTER 2

BEANS

Consider the bean layer of a taco dish to be the taco's second foundation, the creamy layer that precedes the dish's showcase ingredients. While beans certainly can star in their own show, particularly in vegetarian entrées (see chapter on veggies), they are genius in their backup role as well.

I love the rustic addition of a hearty bean spread. Beans lend contrast, both in flavor and texture, and a soulful element.

BEAN RECIPES

PREP TIME: 5 minutes

COOK TIME: 5 minutes

TOTAL TIME: 10 minutes

YIELD: 4 servings

BLACK BEAN SPREAD

1. In a sauté pan, heat oil over medium-high heat. Add onions, garlic, cumin, and black beans.
2. Sauté for about 2 minutes. Then, with a fork, mash black beans until oil is absorbed and black beans become a paste.
3. Season beans with salt and pepper.

INGREDIENTS:

½ cup olive oil

½ cup white onions, diced small

1 tablespoon garlic, minced

½ teaspoon ground cumin

1 pound cooked black beans

1 teaspoon salt

½ teaspoon pepper

BLACK-EYED PEA SPREAD

PREP TIME: 5 minutes

COOK TIME: 5 minutes

TOTAL TIME: 10 minutes

YIELD: 4 servings

INGREDIENTS:

¼ cup vegetable oil

½ cup white onions, diced small

1 tablespoon garlic, minced

1 pound cooked black-eyed peas

1 teaspoon salt

½ teaspoon pepper

1. In a sauté pan, heat oil over medium-high heat. Add onions, garlic, and black-eyed peas.
2. Sauté the peas and aromatics for about 2 minutes. Using a fork, mash black-eyed peas until oil is absorbed and the peas become a paste.
3. Season with salt and pepper. Remove Black-Eyed Pea Spread from heat.

FAVA BEAN SPREAD

PREP TIME: 5 minutes

COOK TIME: 5 minutes

TOTAL TIME: 10 minutes

YIELD: 4 servings

INGREDIENTS:

3 cups chicken stock

1 pound frozen fava beans, thawed

1 tablespoon fresh lemon juice

3 tablespoons fresh mint, chopped

3 tablespoons fresh cilantro, chopped

1 teaspoon kosher salt

1 teaspoon fresh ground black pepper

1. In a medium saucepan, bring chicken stock to a boil over medium-high heat. Add fava beans and reduce heat to medium-low and simmer until beans are tender, about 5 minutes.
2. Drain fava beans, reserving 1 cup of the stock. Place the beans, the reserved stock, and lemon juice in a blender. Add mint and cilantro and blend until smooth. Season with salt and pepper.

GARBANZO BEAN SPREAD

1. In a sauté pan, heat oil over medium-high heat. Add onions, garlic, paprika, and garbanzo beans.
2. Sauté beans for about 2 minutes. Place garbanzo beans in a blender and puree into smooth paste.
3. Add salt and pepper.

PREP TIME: 5 minutes

COOK TIME: 5 minutes

TOTAL TIME: 10 minutes

YIELD: 4 servings

INGREDIENTS:

½ cup vegetable oil

½ cup white onions, diced small

1 tablespoon garlic, minced

½ tablespoon paprika

1 pound cooked garbanzo beans

1 teaspoon salt

½ teaspoon pepper

PINTO BEAN SPREAD

1. In a sauté pan, heat oil over medium-high heat. Add onions, garlic, paprika, and pinto beans.
2. Sauté for about 2 minutes. With a fork, mash pinto beans until oil is absorbed and pinto beans become a paste.
3. Season with salt and pepper. Remove pinto bean puree from heat.

PREP TIME: 5 minutes

COOK TIME: 5 minutes

TOTAL TIME: 10 minutes

YIELD: 4 servings

INGREDIENTS:

½ cup olive oil

½ cup white onions, diced small

1 tablespoon garlic, minced

½ tablespoon paprika

1 pound cooked pinto beans

1 teaspoon salt

½ teaspoon pepper

PREP TIME: 5 minutes

COOK TIME: 5 minutes

TOTAL TIME: 10 minutes

YIELD: 4 servings

WHITE BEAN SPREAD

INGREDIENTS:

¼ cup vegetable oil

¼ cup olive oil

½ cup white onions, diced small

1 tablespoon garlic, minced

1 teaspoon cumin

1 pound cooked white beans

1 teaspoon salt

½ teaspoon pepper

1. In a sauté pan, heat oil over medium-high heat. Add onions, garlic, cumin, and white beans.

2. Sauté for about 2 minutes. With a fork, mash white beans until oil is absorbed and the beans become a paste.

3. Season with salt and pepper. Remove White Bean Spread from heat.

THE TOPPINGS

CHAPTER 3

SAUCES

A blender is a beautiful thing—speedy, efficient, and perfect for a recipe's saucy elements. But when it comes to extracting flavor from ingredients, one rustic, ancient gadget trumps even the most modern and expensive blender: A molcajete, a Mexican mortar and pestle, can be your best accomplice in creating spectacular taco sauces.

Often made of volcanic stone, the molcajete's wide bowl shape allows ingredients to mingle as they are pummeled to a paste or a chunky sauce. A simple clove of garlic transforms into a truly aromatic element as its flavor is released in the molcajete. The same goes for cilantro leaves and stems—untouched, they can be mild, but pummeled in the stone bowl, they release their herbaceous, heady fragrance.

Think of this nifty tool as the secret to outstanding sauces and pastes.

Several of the following recipes call for a molcajete—or any large mortar and pestle—for grinding ingredients. As an alternative, of course, you can follow the recipes' blender method.

A blender, however, is not always a shortcut tool—it's often a necessity. Some sauces in this chapter, such as the Green Cilantro Sauce, are best when blended to achieve a smooth, creamy consistency.

RECEIPES

GREEN CILANTRO SAUCE

PREP TIME: 5 minutes

COOK TIME: 5 minutes

TOTAL TIME: 10 minutes

YIELD: 4 servings

Place all ingredients in a food processor and blend until well combined.

INGREDIENTS:

¾ cup fresh cilantro, finely chopped

juice of 2 whole limes

¼ cup vegetable oil

½ small onion, chopped

1 clove garlic

1 teaspoon chile peppers

1 leaf iceberg lettuce

PREP TIME: 5 minutes

COOK TIME: 5 minutes

TOTAL TIME: 10 minutes

YIELD: 4 servings

GRILLED TOMATO SALSA

INGREDIENTS:

3 tablespoons vegetable oil, plus more for brushing tomatoes

1 red onion, chopped

4 garlic cloves

6 plum tomatoes, cut into halves

2 Serrano chiles, cut in half and seeded

juice of 2 whole limes

salt and pepper, to taste

¼ cup fresh cilantro

1. In a sauté pan, heat 3 tablespoons of oil. Add chopped red onion and garlic and cook until soft.
2. Brush tomatoes and Serrano chiles with additional oil and sprinkle them with salt and pepper to taste. Grill or roast the seasoned tomatoes and Serrano chiles over high heat for 10 to 15 minutes, turning every few minutes, or roast them in a 450F degree oven for 10 to 15 minutes.
3. In a food processor, place all ingredients, adding the cilantro at the end. Pulse a few times. Set aside until ready to use.

PREP TIME: 5 minutes

COOK TIME: 10 minutes

TOTAL TIME: 15 minutes

YIELD: 4 servings

MOLCAJETE SAUCE: CHILE DE ARBOL AND SESAME SEED SAUCE

INGREDIENTS:

12 whole chiles de arbol

2 tablespoons sesame seeds, toasted

1 whole roasted garlic clove

2 teaspoons salt

1 tablespoon chile de arbol water

2 tablespoons distilled white vinegar

1 tablespoon water

1 pinch dried oregano

BEFORE YOU START:

Boil chiles de arbol in water for 5 minutes. Let cool and reserve in water.

MOLCAJETE METHOD:

1. In a molcajete, place chiles, sesame seeds, garlic, salt, and 1 tablespoon of the chile de arbol water.
2. Use pestle to break down ingredients into paste. Add vinegar, water, and dried oregano and combine well.

BLENDER METHOD:

In a blender, blend chiles, sesame seeds, garlic, salt, 1 tablespoon of the chile de arbol water, vinegar, and water on high speed until ingredients are well combined. Add oregano and blend for another 10 seconds.

MOLCAJETE SAUCE: CHILE DE ARBOL SAUCE

PREP TIME: 5 minutes

COOK TIME: 5 minutes

TOTAL TIME: 10 minutes

YIELD: 4 servings

BEFORE YOU START:

Boil chiles de arbol in water for 5 minutes. Let cool and reserve in water.

MOLCAJETE METHOD:

1. In a molcajete, place chiles, garlic, salt, and 1 tablespoon of the chile de arbol water.
2. Use pestle to break down ingredients into sauce. Add vinegar and water and combine well.

BLENDER METHOD:

In a blender, blend chiles, garlic, salt, 1 tablespoon of the chile de arbol water, vinegar, and water on high speed until ingredients are well combined.

INGREDIENTS:

12 whole chiles de arbol

1 whole garlic clove, roasted

2 teaspoons salt

1 tablespoon chile de arbol water

1 ounce white vinegar

1 ounce water

PREP TIME: 5 minutes

COOK TIME: 5 minutes

TOTAL TIME: 10 minutes

YIELD: 4 servings

MOLCAJETE SAUCE: COOKED GREEN TOMATILLO SAUCE

INGREDIENTS:

2 tomatillos

½ green jalapeño pepper

2 teaspoon salt

3 sprigs cilantro, plus chopped cilantro for garnish

1 tablespoon shallots, minced, for garnish

BEFORE YOU START:

1. Boil tomatillos in water for 5 minutes. Let cool and reserve in water.
2. Boil jalapeño in water for 5 minutes. Let cool. Remove seeds and reserve water.

MOLCAJETE METHOD:

1. In a molcajete, place tomatillos, jalapeño, and salt.
2. Use pestle to break down ingredients into sauce. Add cilantro and combine well.
3. To serve, garnish with shallots and chopped cilantro.

BLENDER METHOD:

In a blender, blend tomatillos, jalapeño, and salt on medium speed until ingredients are well combined. Add cilantro and blend for another 10 seconds. To serve, garnish with shallots and chopped cilantro.

MOLCAJETE SAUCE: COOKED TOMATO AND CHILE DE ARBOL SAUCE

PREP TIME: 5 minutes

COOK TIME: 5 minutes

TOTAL TIME: 10 minutes

YIELD: 4 servings

BEFORE YOU START:

1. Boil chiles de arbol in water for 5 minutes. Let cool and reserve in water.
2. Boil tomato in water for 5 minutes. Let cool and reserve in water.

MOLCAJETE METHOD:

1. In a molcajete, place chiles, salt, and tomato.
2. Use pestle to break down ingredients into sauce. Add cilantro and combine well.

BLENDER METHOD:

In a blender, blend chiles, salt, and tomato on medium speed until ingredients are well combined. Add cilantro and blend for another 10 seconds.

INGREDIENTS:

2 whole chiles de arbol

1 teaspoon salt

1 whole tomato

2 sprigs cilantro

PREP TIME: 5 minutes
COOK TIME: 5 minutes
TOTAL TIME: 10 minutes
YIELD: 4 servings

MOLCAJETE SAUCE: COOKED TOMATO AND GRILLED TOMATILLO SAUCE

INGREDIENTS:

2 whole chiles de arbol

1½ whole tomatoes

1 teaspoon salt

1½ tomatillos

½ teaspoon coconut vinegar

1 sprig cilantro

1 pinch dried oregano

BEFORE YOU START:

1. Boil chiles de arbol in water for 5 minutes. Let cool and reserve in water.
2. Boil tomatoes in water for 5 minutes. Let cool and reserve in water.
3. Grill tomatillos until charred on all sides.

MOLCAJETE METHOD:

1. In a molcajete, place chiles, tomatoes, and salt.
2. Use pestle to break down ingredients into sauce. Add tomatillos and combine well.
3. Add vinegar, cilantro, and oregano and combine well.

BLENDER METHOD:

In a blender, blend chiles, tomatoes, and salt on medium speed until ingredients are well combined. Add tomatillos and vinegar and blend. Add cilantro and oregano and blend for another 10 seconds.

MOLCAJETE SAUCE: GRILLED GREEN TOMATILLO SAUCE

PREP TIME: 5 minutes

COOK TIME: 5 minutes

TOTAL TIME: 10 minutes

YIELD: 4 servings

BEFORE YOU START:

1. Boil tomatillos in water for 5 minutes. Let cool and reserve in water.
2. Boil jalapeño in water for 5 minutes. Let cool. Remove seeds.
3. Grill whole tomatillo until charred on all sides.
4. Grill jalapeño until charred on all sides.

MOLCAJETE METHOD:

1. In a molcajete, place boiled tomatillos, boiled jalapeño, and salt in molcajete.
2. Use pestle to break down ingredients into sauce.
3. Add grilled tomatillo, grilled jalapeño, and onion and combine well. Add cilantro and combine well.

BLENDER METHOD:

1. In a blender, blend boiled tomatillos, boiled jalapeño, and salt on medium speed until ingredients are well combined.
2. Add grilled tomatillo, grilled jalapeño, and onion and combine well. Add cilantro and blend for another 10 seconds.

INGREDIENTS:

2 whole tomatillos, to boil

½ green jalapeño pepper, to boil

2 teaspoons salt

1 whole tomatillo, to grill

½ green jalapeño, to grill

1 tablespoon grilled onion

3 sprigs cilantro

PREP TIME: 5 minutes

COOK TIME: 5 minutes

TOTAL TIME: 10 minutes

YIELD: 4 servings

MOLCAJETE SAUCE: TOMATO SAUCE

INGREDIENTS:

2 whole chiles de arbol

1 whole tomato, to boil

1 whole tomato, to grill

2 teaspoons salt

1 whole garlic clove, roasted

1 tablespoon grilled onion

2 sprigs cilantro

BEFORE YOU START:

1. In a pan over high heat, toast chiles de arbol to release oils.
2. Boil tomato in water for 5 minutes. Let cool and reserve in water.
3. Grill tomato until charred on all sides.

MOLCAJETE METHOD:

1. In a molcajete, place chiles, tomatoes, and salt.
2. Use pestle to break down ingredients into sauce.
3. Add garlic, onion, and cilantro, combine well.

BLENDER METHOD:

In a blender, blend chiles, tomatoes, and salt on medium speed until ingredients are well combined. Add garlic, onion, and cilantro and combine well.

SPICY MANGO SAUCE

1. In a saucepan, combine mango, water, and sugar and cook over medium-low heat until softened, about 10 minutes. Set aside to cool.
2. In a blender, place the cooled mango-water-and-sugar mixture. Add the remaining ingredients and blend until smooth and set aside until ready to use.

PREP TIME: 5 minutes
COOK TIME: 12 minutes
TOTAL TIME: 17 minutes
YIELD: 4 servings

INGREDIENTS:

2 cups ripe mango, peeled and cubed

1½ cups water

1 tablespoon sugar

4 tablespoons ají rocoto

1 tablespoon coconut vinegar

½ tablespoon vegetable oil

2 teaspoons kosher salt

1 tablespoon lemon juice

SPICY PEACH CHIPOTLE SAUCE

1. In a small saucepan, cook sugar in ¼ cup of water over medium-high heat for 10 minutes until reduced.
2. In a medium-size pan, char chipotle to release oils. To the same pan, add peaches and garlic and cook until garlic is golden. Add the remaining 1 cup of water. Cook on low heat for 20 minutes until peppers are rehydrated. Let cool.
3. Add all ingredients to blender and blend until creamy.

PREP TIME: 5 minutes
COOK TIME: 25 minutes
TOTAL TIME: 30 minutes
YIELD: 4 servings

INGREDIENTS:

¼ cup sugar

1¼ cup water

2 whole chipotle peppers, dried

6 whole fresh peaches, peeled and chopped

1 tablespoon garlic

2 tablespoons vegetable oil

2 teaspoons kosher salt

SALSA VERDE

SALSA VERDE CRUDA

In a blender, combine all ingredients and mix until liquid.

PREP TIME: 5 minutes
COOK TIME: 5 minutes
TOTAL TIME: 10 minutes
YIELD: 4 servings

INGREDIENTS:

2–3 whole baby lettuce leaves or spinach leaves

¼ jalapeño

1 whole green onion

2 teaspoons salt

2 whole tomatillos, quartered

5 sprigs cilantro

PREP TIME: 5 minutes

COOK TIME: 5 minutes

TOTAL TIME: 10 minutes

YIELD: 4 servings

TOMATO SALSA CRUDA

INGREDIENTS:

2 whole tomatoes, quartered

¼ jalapeño

1 whole green onion

2 teaspoons salt

2 tablespoons olive oil

3–4 fresh oregano leaves

In a blender, combine tomatoes, jalapeño, onion, and salt. Blend until liquid. Add oil and oregano, then blend another 10 seconds.

PREP TIME: 5 minutes
COOK TIME: 5 minutes
TOTAL TIME: 10 minutes
YIELD: 4 servings

SPICY ROCOTO SAUCE

Place all ingredients in a food processor. Blend until well combined.

INGREDIENTS:

½ cup rocoto peppers, fresh

3 tablespoons vegetable oil

juice of 2 whole limes

3 sprigs cilantro or parsley

CHAPTER 4

PICOS

There's so much more to pico than a few chopped tomatoes, onions, and chiles. In this chapter, you'll find more than a dozen chunky, flavor-packed ways to accessorize your new-style tacos. Picos are as versatile as the ingredients in your fridge's crisper drawer. Make them hot or sweet—or hot *and* sweet. Make them tangy, herbaceous, and always fresh.

In this chapter, we'll make a Brazilian pico that's packed with bell peppers and jalapeños, a cherry-pepper-studded pico, a kicky corn-and-poblano pico, a minty avocado pico, a Peruvian corn pico, an herby pico verde, a sweet-spicy pineapple pico, a hot Serrano pico, a spicy peach-corn pico, and a refreshing cucumber-tomato pico.

One important pico tip: Dice or chop your ingredients equally in size. This way you'll maximize the flavors of your pico and avoid getting too much of one ingredient and too little of another in any single bite.

A word about Venezuelan-style guasacaca sauces: Once you've discovered them, you'll want to spoon them on everything. This is a sauce that's always within reach at my house when the grill is fired up—you can add it to pretty much anything you put on the grill. Guasacaca gets its luxurious qualities from avocados and its flavor punch from aromatics and herbs. But before you call it guacamole, know that this sauce is also thinner and zestier than your classic guac. It's also more acidic, because it combines both lime juice and vinegar for its bright nature.

Speaking of acidity, it's important to select your mixing bowl carefully. The recipes that contain acidic ingredients like citrus juices or tomatoes are best prepared in nonreactive bowls (such as glass, ceramic, stainless steel, or enamel-coated cast iron). This prevents your sauce from picking up that metallic taste that's often generated when acidic ingredients meet metals such as copper, aluminum, and iron.

PICO RECIPES

PREP TIME: 5 minutes

COOK TIME: 20 minutes

TOTAL TIME: 25 minutes

YIELD: 4 servings

PICO DE GALLO

1. In a nonreactive bowl, toss tomatoes, onion, jalapeño, and cilantro with lemon juice and vegetable oil. Season with salt and pepper.
2. Let pico de gallo sit at room temperature for 15–20 minutes before serving.

INGREDIENTS:

2 ripe tomatoes, diced small

½ white onion, diced small

1 red jalapeño, diced small

2 tablespoons fresh cilantro, finely chopped

2 tablespoons lemon juice

½ tablespoon vegetable oil

kosher salt

fresh ground black pepper

PREP TIME: 5 minutes

COOK TIME: 20 minutes

TOTAL TIME: 25 minutes

YIELD: 4 servings

BRAZILIAN PICO DE GALLO

1. In a nonreactive bowl, place tomatoes, peppers, onions, jalapeño, and parsley. Toss with vinegar, lemon juice, olive oil, and water. Season with salt.
2. Let pico sit at room temperature for 15–20 minutes before serving.

INGREDIENTS:

2 whole ripe tomatoes, diced small

½ cup green bell pepper, diced small

½ cup red bell pepper, diced small

2 yellow onions, diced small

1 red jalapeño, diced small

3 tablespoons fresh flat-leaf parsley, finely chopped

4 tablespoons distilled white vinegar

2 tablespoons lemon juice

3 tablespoons extra-virgin olive oil

3 tablespoons water

1 teaspoon kosher salt

PREP TIME: 5 minutes

COOK TIME: 20 minutes

TOTAL TIME: 25 minutes

YIELD: 4 servings

CHERRY PEPPER PICO DE GALLO

INGREDIENTS:

24 fresh whole sweet cherry peppers, seeded and diced small

⅓ cup shallots, diced small

2 tablespoons cilantro, finely chopped

1 teaspoon garlic, minced

1 teaspoon kosher salt

1 teaspoon fresh black pepper

¼ cup coconut vinegar

¼ cup olive oil

¼ cup vegetable oil

Toss all ingredients together in a nonreactive bowl. Set pico aside for 20 minutes before serving.

PREP TIME: 5 minutes

COOK TIME: 10 minutes

TOTAL TIME: 15 minutes

YIELD: 4 servings

CORN POBLANO PICO DE GALLO

In a nonreactive bowl, toss tomatoes, corn, poblano peppers, onion, jalapeño, and cilantro with lemon juice and vegetable oil. Season with salt and pepper. Set aside at room temperature for 15–20 minutes before serving.

INGREDIENTS:

2 whole ripe tomatoes, diced small

1 cup corn kernels, grilled

½ cup poblano peppers, diced small

½ white onion, diced small

1 red jalapeño, diced small

2 tablespoons fresh cilantro, finely chopped

2 tablespoons lemon juice

½ tablespoon vegetable oil

kosher salt

fresh ground black pepper

PREP TIME: 5 minutes

COOK TIME: 20 minutes

TOTAL TIME: 25 minutes

YIELD: 4 servings

MINT AVOCADO PICO DE GALLO

INGREDIENTS:

2 ripe tomatoes, diced small

1 whole avocado, diced small

½ white onion, diced small

1 red jalapeño, diced small

2 tablespoons fresh cilantro, finely chopped

2 tablespoons fresh mint, finely chopped

2 tablespoons lemon juice

½ tablespoon vegetable oil

kosher salt

fresh ground black pepper

1. In a nonreactive bowl, toss tomatoes, avocado, onion, jalapeño, cilantro, and mint with lemon juice and vegetable oil. Season with salt and pepper.
2. Set aside and let pico de gallo sit at room temperature for 15–20 minutes before serving.

PERUVIAN CORN PICO DE GALLO

PREP TIME: 5 minutes
COOK TIME: 20 minutes
TOTAL TIME: 25 minutes
YIELD: 4 servings

1. In a nonreactive bowl, toss tomatoes, Peruvian corn, onion, jalapeño, and cilantro with lemon juice and vegetable oil. Season with salt and pepper.
2. Let pico de gallo sit at room temperature for 15–20 minutes before serving.

INGREDIENTS:

2 ripe tomatoes, diced small

½ cup Peruvian corn, cooked or steamed

½ white onion, diced small

1 red jalapeño, diced small

2 tablespoons fresh cilantro, finely chopped

2 tablespoons lemon juice

½ tablespoon vegetable oil

kosher salt

fresh ground black pepper

PREP TIME: 5 minutes

COOK TIME: 20 minutes

TOTAL TIME: 25 minutes

YIELD: 4 servings

PICO VERDE

INGREDIENTS:

¼ cup leeks, white part only, diced small

1 whole poblano pepper, seeded and diced small

1 whole Anaheim pepper, seeded and diced small

1 whole green jalapeño pepper, seeded and diced small

1 whole tomatillo, seeded and diced small

2 tablespoons fresh cilantro, finely chopped

2 tablespoons fresh Italian parsley, finely chopped

1 tablespoon fresh mint, finely chopped

1 teaspoon fresh thyme, finely chopped

½ cup white vinegar

¼ cup olive oil

¼ cup vegetable oil

Toss all ingredients together in a nonreactive bowl. Combine well and let bowl stand for 20 minutes before serving pico.

PINEAPPLE PICO DE GALLO

PREP TIME: 5 minutes

COOK TIME: 20 minutes

TOTAL TIME: 25 minutes

YIELD: 4 servings

1. In a nonreactive bowl, toss tomatoes, onion, jalapeño, pineapple, and cilantro with lemon juice and vegetable oil. Season with salt and pepper.
2. Let pico sit at room temperature for 15–20 minutes before serving.

INGREDIENTS:

2 whole ripe tomatoes, diced small

½ white onion, diced small

1 whole red jalapeño, diced small

½ cup pineapple, diced small

2 tablespoons fresh cilantro, finely chopped

2 tablespoons lemon juice

½ tablespoon vegetable oil

kosher salt

fresh ground black pepper

PREP TIME: 5 minutes

COOK TIME: 20 minutes

TOTAL TIME: 25 minutes

YIELD: 4 servings

SERRANO PICO DE GALLO

INGREDIENTS:

4 large tomatoes, about 2½ pounds, seeded and roughly chopped

1 cup white onion, chopped

5 teaspoons garlic, minced

4 Serrano chiles, seeds and stems removed, minced

¼ cup fresh cilantro, chopped

2 tablespoons fresh lime juice

½ teaspoon kosher salt

Toss together all ingredients in a nonreactive bowl and set aside until ready to use.

SPICY PEACH, CORN, AND TOMATO PICO DE GALLO

PREP TIME: 5 minutes

COOK TIME: 20 minutes

TOTAL TIME: 25 minutes

YIELD: 4 servings

Toss together all ingredients in a nonreactive bowl. Combine well and let bowl sit for 20 minutes before serving pico.

INGREDIENTS:

1 whole fresh cayenne pepper, diced small

¾ cup peaches, grilled and diced small

½ cup corn kernels, grilled

½ cup fresh tomatoes, diced small

¼ cup fresh cilantro, finely chopped

½ tablespoon fresh mint, finely chopped

juice of 1 whole lime

1 tablespoon white vinegar

¼ cup olive oil

1 teaspoon kosher salt

1 teaspoon sugar

PREP TIME: 5 minutes

COOK TIME: 15 minutes

TOTAL TIME: 20 minutes

YIELD: 4 servings

SPICY CUCUMBER TOMATO PICO DE GALLO

INGREDIENTS:

2 whole ripe tomatoes, diced small

1 cup cucumber, diced small

½ red onion, diced small

1 red jalapeño, diced small

2 tablespoons fresh cilantro, finely chopped

2 tablespoons lemon juice

½ tablespoon vegetable oil

kosher salt

fresh ground black pepper

In a nonreactive bowl, toss together tomatoes, cucumber, onion, jalapeño, and cilantro with lemon juice and vegetable oil. Season with salt and pepper. Let pico sit at room temperature for 15–20 minutes before serving.

SPICY PEPPER SALSA

PREP TIME: 5 minutes
COOK TIME: 30 minutes
TOTAL TIME: 35 minutes
YIELD: 4 servings

1. In a nonreactive bowl, whisk together sugar, coconut vinegar, and white vinegar until sugar has dissolved.
2. Fold in the chile cachucha, cayenne peppers, red onion, garlic, lemon juice, salt, and both vegetable and olive oil.
3. Let salsa sit for 30 minutes before serving, or place in an airtight jar for up to 4 weeks.

INGREDIENTS:

1 tablespoon sugar

¼ cup coconut vinegar

½ cup white distilled vinegar

1 cup chile cachucha, diced small

2 fresh cayenne peppers, diced small

¼ cup red onion, diced small

1 teaspoon garlic, minced

juice of 1 whole fresh lemon

1½ teaspoons kosher salt

2 tablespoons vegetable oil

1 tablespoon olive oil

PREP TIME: 5 minutes
COOK TIME: 10 minutes
TOTAL TIME: 15 minutes
YIELD: 4 servings

GUASACACA

INGREDIENTS:

3 Hass avocados, diced small

1 small red onion, diced small

3 green onions, diced small

2 garlic cloves, minced

1 red bell pepper, diced small

1 green bell pepper, diced small

1 leek, white part only, diced small

3 limes, juiced

2 tablespoons white vinegar

1 cup olive oil or vegetable oil

1 bunch fresh cilantro, finely chopped

1 tablespoon kosher salt

1 teaspoon sugar

1 teaspoon black pepper

Toss all ingredients together in a nonreactive bowl and set aside for 10 minutes before serving. If not using right away, refrigerate until ready to use.

SPICY GUASACACA

Toss together all the ingredients in a nonreactive bowl and set aside for 10 minutes until ready to use. If not serving right away, refrigerate the sauce until you are ready to enjoy it.

PREP TIME: 5 minutes

COOK TIME: 10 minutes

TOTAL TIME: 15 minutes

YIELD: 4 servings

INGREDIENTS:

3 Hass avocados, diced small

1 green jalapeño pepper, diced small

1 green jalapeño pepper, seeded, deveined, and diced small

1 small red onion, diced small

3 green onions, diced small

2 garlic cloves, minced

1 red bell pepper, diced small

1 green bell pepper, diced small

1 leek, white part only, diced small

juice of 3 limes

2 tablespoons white vinegar

1 cup olive oil or vegetable oil

1 bunch fresh cilantro, finely chopped

1 tablespoon kosher salt

1 teaspoon sugar

1 teaspoon black pepper

PREP TIME: 5 minutes

COOK TIME: 10 minutes

TOTAL TIME: 15 minutes

YIELD: 4 servings

GREEN GUASACACA

INGREDIENTS:

1 small red onion, diced small

3 green onions, diced small

2 garlic cloves, minced

2 green bell peppers, diced small

1 leek, white part only, diced small

juice of 3 limes

2 tablespoons white vinegar

1 cup olive oil or vegetable oil

1 bunch fresh cilantro, finely chopped

1 bunch Italian parsley, finely chopped

1 tablespoon fresh oregano, finely chopped

1 tablespoon kosher salt

1 teaspoon sugar

1 teaspoon black pepper

Toss all the ingredients together in a nonreactive bowl and set it aside for 10 minutes before serving. If not serving right away, refrigerate sauce until ready to use.

CHAPTER 5

PICKLED RECIPES

A taco is not fully dressed without a worthy side of pickled vegetables or fresh-made salsa. Pickled onions, radishes, and other veggies add that delightfully briny component to a taco dish. In the flavor layers that make up any of our "New Taco Classics" combos, there's always room for a touch of lovely acidity. And this is what the following recipes bring to the taco party.

RECIPES

PICKLED ONIONS

In a small bowl, stir together the onions, vinegar, agave, cilantro, and olive oil. Season with salt and pepper, and let mixture sit at room temperature for 1 hour.

PREP TIME: 10 minutes

COOK TIME: 1 hour

TOTAL TIME: 1 hour, 10 minutes

YIELD: 4 servings

INGREDIENTS:

¾ cup red onion, thinly sliced

¼ cup red wine vinegar

1 tablespoon agave syrup

1 tablespoon fresh cilantro, finely chopped

2 tablespoons olive oil

kosher salt, to taste

black pepper, to taste

LIME PICKLED ONIONS

In a bowl, whisk together the lime juice, vinegar, sugar, vegetable oil, salt, and pepper. Add the red onions and cilantro or parsley. Refrigerate for at least 30 minutes before serving.

PREP TIME: 10 minutes

COOK TIME: 30 minutes

TOTAL TIME: 40 minutes

YIELD: 4 servings

INGREDIENTS:

3 tablespoons lime juice

2 tablespoons distilled white vinegar

½ tablespoon sugar

1 tablespoon vegetable oil

1 teaspoon kosher salt

1 teaspoon pepper

1 cup red onions (packed), thinly sliced

1 tablespoon fresh cilantro or parsley, finely chopped

SPICY PICKLED ONIONS

PREP TIME: 10 minutes

COOK TIME: 1 hour

TOTAL TIME: 1 hour, 10 minutes

YIELD: 4 servings

INGREDIENTS:

¾ cup red onions, thinly sliced

¼ cup red wine vinegar

1 tablespoon agave syrup

2 tablespoons olive oil

1 tablespoon fresh cilantro, finely chopped

1 large red jalapeño, thinly sliced

kosher salt

black pepper

In a small bowl, stir together the onions, vinegar, agave, olive oil, cilantro, and red jalapeño. Season with salt and pepper, and let the mixture sit at room temperature for 1 hour before serving.

PICKLED WATERMELON RADISH

PREP TIME: 10 minutes

COOK TIME: 10 minutes

TOTAL TIME: 20 minutes

YIELD: 4 servings

INGREDIENTS:

1 cup watermelon radish, thinly sliced

⅓ cup coconut vinegar

1 cup water

1 tablespoon agave syrup

1 teaspoon kosher salt

1 teaspoon dry mustard

1. Place radishes in medium-size airtight jar.
2. In a bowl, whisk together the vinegar, water, agave, salt, and mustard. Pour the liquid over the radishes. Cover and refrigerate jar for at least 1 hour until ready to use.

PREP TIME: 10 minutes

COOK TIME: 10 minutes

TOTAL TIME: 20 minutes

YIELD: 4 servings

SALSA CRIOLLA

1. In a medium-size bowl, add the onions with 3 tablespoons of the salt. Stir to combine and set bowl aside for 10 minutes.

2. Pour the onions into a sieve and rinse them well under cool water. Let them drain well.

3. Place drained onions in a bowl. Season them with the remaining 1 teaspoon of salt and pepper. Add oil and stir to combine well.

4. Add ají amarillo, lime juice, vinegar, and cilantro. Stir to combine and allow salsa to sit for 10 minutes so the flavors can meld.

5. Before serving the salsa, adjust seasonings, if necessary.

INGREDIENTS:

2 whole red onions, thinly sliced

4 teaspoons kosher salt, divided

½ teaspoon black pepper

1 tablespoon olive oil

1 whole ají amarillo, thinly sliced

2 whole limes, juiced

2 tablespoons coconut vinegar

¼ cup fresh cilantro, finely chopped

PERUVIAN CORN SALSA CRIOLLA

PREP TIME: 10 minutes

COOK TIME: 20 minutes

TOTAL TIME: 30 minutes

YIELD: 4 servings

INGREDIENTS:

2 red onions

¼ cup fresh lemon juice

¼ cup white vinegar

¼ cup sugar

1 cup cooked Peruvian corn, cooked (or steamed)

1½ teaspoons kosher salt

¼ cup fresh cilantro

1. Using a mandolin, slice the onions.
2. In a mixing bowl, whisk together the lemon juice, vinegar, and sugar until all ingredients are well combined. Fold in Peruvian corn.
3. Add the onions, salt, and cilantro to the mixing bowl and stir to combine. Let the salsa sit at room temperature for at least 20 minutes before serving.

ONIONS AGRIDOLCE

PREP TIME: 10 minutes

COOK TIME: 30 minutes

TOTAL TIME: 40 minutes

YIELD: 4 servings

INGREDIENTS:

⅓ cup rice vinegar

⅓ cup agave syrup

1 teaspoon kosher salt

1 teaspoon pepper

1 cup red onions (packed), thinly sliced

½ tablespoon of fresh cilantro or parsley, finely chopped

1. In a bowl, whisk together the vinegar, agave, salt, and pepper.
2. Add the red onions and cilantro or parsley and stir to combine ingredients. Refrigerate for at least 30 minutes before serving.

CHAPTER 6

CREMAS

I love whisking up a flavorful crema (cream) to top one of my taco dishes. Cremas are all about adding contrast and a touch of luxury to the combo of taco ingredients. It's that creamy layer that contrasts with a crisp fried tortilla or a crunchy slaw.

I've simplified the process for you by creating variations of cremas that use the same or a similar base. To this base, we can add, subtract, or substitute ingredients to give each crema its own flavor profile.

Quick tip: If you find that the crema becomes too thick after storing it in the fridge, whisk in 1 or 2 tablespoons of water to restore its full creaminess.

CREMAS RECIPES

AVOCADO CREMA

Place avocado, lime juice, sour cream, water, heavy cream, salt, and pepper in a blender and blend ingredients until well combined, about 1 minute.

PREP TIME: 5 minutes
COOK TIME: 2 minutes
TOTAL TIME: 7 minutes
YIELD: 4 servings

INGREDIENTS:

1 whole avocado

2 tablespoons lime juice

¼ cup sour cream

½ cup water

½ cup heavy cream

1 teaspoon kosher salt

½ teaspoon pepper

BLUE CHEESE CREMA

In a blender, add blue cheese, lemon juice, lemon zest, mayonnaise, salt, and pepper. Blend mixture on high until well combined. Add water as needed to achieve creamy consistency.

PREP TIME: 5 minutes
COOK TIME: 2 minutes
TOTAL TIME: 7 minutes
YIELD: 4 servings

INGREDIENTS:

½ cup blue cheese crumbles

juice of 1 whole lemon

zest of 1 whole lemon

¼ cup mayonnaise

1 pinch kosher salt

½ teaspoon fresh black pepper

2 tablespoons water

PREP TIME: 5 minutes

COOK TIME: 10 minutes

TOTAL TIME: 15 minutes

YIELD: 4 servings

INGREDIENTS:

½ cup Greek yogurt

1 tablespoon sour cream

2 tablespoons heavy cream

1 whole chipotle in adobo

1 teaspoon adobo liquid

1 teaspoon lime juice

1 teaspoon kosher salt

CHIPOTLE CREMA

In a blender, place Greek yogurt, sour cream, heavy cream, chipotle, adobo liquid, lime juice, and salt and blend until well combined, about 1 minute.

PREP TIME: 5 minutes

COOK TIME: 5 minutes

TOTAL TIME: 10 minutes

YIELD: 8 servings

INGREDIENTS:

6 large garlic cloves, or heads of garlic, roasted

2 large Hass avocados, peeled and pitted

1 tablespoon fresh lime juice

1 large red bell pepper, roasted, peeled and destemmed

13½ ounces canned coconut milk

kosher salt

COCONUT AVOCADO CREMA

In a blender, place all ingredients and blend until smooth.

CITRUS CREMA

In a blender, place Greek yogurt, sour cream, lemon juice, lime juice, orange juice, salt, and pepper and blend until smooth and well combined, about 1 minute. Pour crema into a bowl and fold in lemon zest and lime zest.

PREP TIME: 5 minutes
COOK TIME: 5 minutes
TOTAL TIME: 10 minutes
YIELD: 4 servings

INGREDIENTS:

½ cup Greek yogurt

¼ cup sour cream

2 tablespoons lemon juice

1 tablespoon lime juice

1 tablespoon orange juice

1 teaspoon kosher salt

½ teaspoon black pepper

zest of 1 lemon

zest of 1 lime

LEMON CREMA

Place Greek yogurt, sour cream, lemon juice, salt, and pepper in a blender and blend until well combined, about 1 minute. Pour crema into a bowl and stir in lemon zest.

PREP TIME: 5 minutes
COOK TIME: 5 minutes
TOTAL TIME: 10 minutes
YIELD: 4 servings

INGREDIENTS:

½ cup Greek yogurt

¼ cup sour cream

4 tablespoons lemon juice

1 teaspoon salt

½ teaspoon black pepper

zest of 1 lemon

LIME CREMA

PREP TIME: 5 minutes

COOK TIME: 5 minutes

TOTAL TIME: 10 minutes

YIELD: 4 servings

INGREDIENTS:

½ cup Greek yogurt

¼ cup sour cream

4 tablespoons lime juice

1 teaspoon kosher salt

½ teaspoon black pepper

zest of 1 lime

In a blender, place Greek yogurt, sour cream, lime juice, salt, and pepper and blend until well combined, about 1 minute. Pour crema into a bowl and fold in the lime zest.

BASIL-SPINACH CREMA

PREP TIME: 5 minutes

COOK TIME: 10 minutes

TOTAL TIME: 15 minutes

YIELD: 8 servings

INGREDIENTS:

½ cup sour cream

½ cup mayonnaise

¼ cup packed basil, chopped

¼ cup packed cilantro, chopped

1 cup packed spinach, chopped

juice of 1 lemon

1 teaspoon kosher salt

½ teaspoon pepper

In a blender, combine all ingredients. Blend until smooth.

PREP TIME: 5 minutes

COOK TIME: 20 minutes

TOTAL TIME: 25 minutes

YIELD: 8 servings

AJÍ AMARILLO CREMA

1. In a skillet, heat 2 tablespoons of the olive oil over medium-high heat. Add onions, garlic, and the white part of the scallions. Sauté until onions are translucent.
2. Place the sautéed ingredients in a blender. Add mayonnaise, ají amarillo paste, the remaining 2 tablespoons of olive oil, lemon juice, queso fresco, salt, and pepper. Blend until smooth.
3. Pour crema into a serving bowl and garnish with the green scallions.

INGREDIENTS:

4 tablespoons olive oil, divided

⅓ cup onions, diced small

3 garlic cloves, minced

3 scallions, minced (separate the white and green parts)

½ cup mayonnaise

½ tablespoon ají amarillo paste

juice of 1 lemon

½ cup queso fresco

1 teaspoon kosher salt

½ teaspoon black pepper

ROASTED GARLIC CREMA

PREP TIME: 10 minutes

COOK TIME: 1 hour

TOTAL TIME: 1 hour, 10 minutes

YIELD: 8 servings

1. Preheat oven to 300F degrees. Cut top of garlic heads to expose cloves. Coat garlic with olive oil, salt, and pepper and wrap in aluminum foil.
2. Roast for 45 minutes to 1 hour or until golden brown and soft.
3. Remove garlic from oven and set aside to cool. Squeeze garlic cloves out into a medium bowl.
4. Mash garlic cloves with fork. Add sour cream, lime juice, olive oil, and a pinch of salt and pepper. Whisk together and add heavy cream. Whisk until well combined.

NOTE: Water can be added to achieve desired consistency.

INGREDIENTS:

2 heads of garlic

2 tablespoons olive oil

½ cup sour cream

1 tablespoon lime juice

1 tablespoon olive oil

kosher salt

freshly ground black pepper

2 tablespoons heavy cream

CHILE-LIME CREMA

In a blender, combine all ingredients. Blend until smooth.

PREP TIME: 5 minutes

COOK TIME: 5 minutes

TOTAL TIME: 10 minutes

YIELD: 8 servings

INGREDIENTS:

1 cup sour cream

1 teaspoon chile piquín or chile de arbol

juice of 1 lime

1 teaspoon lime zest

CILANTRO CREMA

In a blender, combine all ingredients. Blend until smooth.

PREP TIME: 5 minutes

COOK TIME: 5 minutes

TOTAL TIME: 10 minutes

YIELD: 8 servings

INGREDIENTS:

2 cups cilantro, with stems

1 cup (packed) spinach

½ cup mayonnaise

juice of 1 lemon

½ avocado, peeled

CHAPTER 7

SLAWS

The beautiful thing about slaws is they add both texture and a delicious acidity to a taco. That texture comes courtesy of a variety of sturdy, crunchy cabbages, from green cabbage to red cabbage to Napa cabbage.

Of course slaw is not made of cabbage alone—in fact, sometimes cabbage isn't even required, as you'll see in the following recipes. We'll make slaw from freshly chopped kale, shredded green papaya, and even julienned jícama. These ingredients share the required crunch factor as well as the ability to withstand both creamy and vinaigrette-style dressings.

A good slaw cleanses your palate and gives freshness to the entire taco dish. It can stand in as a side dish or a topping. And it's a genius way to bulk up your tacos and make them healthier at the same time.

Feel free to experiment with slaw ingredients, to mix and match combinations of veggies and dressings.

A note about cabbage prep: Use a mandolin-style slicer on its thinnest setting to shave and shred cabbages and other veggies. Make ahead: Slice the cabbage, jícama, or chayote up to three days before use and keep it in a bowl or sealable bag with water and some ice cubes. This will keep the veggies super-crunchy until you're ready to use them.

RECIPES

BLUE CHEESE SLAW

MAKE THE BLUE CHEESE CREMA:

In a blender, add blue cheese, lemon juice, lemon zest, mayonnaise, salt, and pepper. Blend mixture on high until well combined. Add water as needed to achieve creamy consistency. Set Blue Cheese Crema aside.

MAKE THE SLAW:

In a medium-size bowl, combine green cabbage, red cabbage, and carrots. Add green onions and celery leaves. Toss with ½ cup of blue cheese crema. Season slaw with salt and pepper.

INGREDIENTS:

FOR THE SLAW:

½ cup green cabbage, shaved

½ cup red cabbage, shaved

¼ cup carrots, julienned

1 tablespoon green onions, green part only, thinly sliced

1 tablespoon celery leaves, thinly sliced

Blue Cheese Crema (see recipe below)

1 teaspoon salt

½ teaspoon pepper

FOR THE BLUE CHEESE CREMA:

½ cup blue cheese crumbles

juice of 1 whole lemon

zest of 1 whole lemon

¼ cup mayonnaise

1 pinch kosher salt

½ teaspoon freshly ground black pepper

2 tablespoons water

CHAYOTE JALAPEÑO SLAW

INGREDIENTS:

FOR THE SLAW:

2 cups chayote, julienned (see prep note)

¼ cup carrots, julienned

1 tablespoon red onions, thinly sliced

1 tablespoon celery leaves, finely chopped

1 tablespoon fresh cilantro, finely chopped

1 tablespoon fresh mint, finely chopped

¼ cup jalapeño, thinly sliced

1 teaspoon salt

½ teaspoon pepper

FOR THE SLAW DRESSING:

½ cup low-fat Greek yogurt

¼ cup mayonnaise

1 tablespoon rice vinegar

½ tablespoon lime juice

1 teaspoon lime zest

½ teaspoon minced garlic

2 teaspoons Dijon mustard

2 teaspoons salt

MAKE THE DRESSING:

In a medium-size bowl, combine all dressing ingredients and mix well.

MAKE THE SLAW:

In a medium-size bowl, combine chayote, carrots, and red onions. Add celery leaves, cilantro, mint, and jalapeños. Toss with ½ cup of slaw dressing. Season slaw with salt and pepper.

PREP NOTE: Cut the chayote in half and remove the middle seed with a spoon, then cut in thin julienne-style strips.

TOTAL TIME: 20 minutes

YIELD: 2 cups

CLASSIC COLESLAW

MAKE SLAW DRESSING:

In a medium-size bowl, combine all dressing ingredients and mix well.

MAKE SLAW:

In a medium-size bowl, combine green cabbage, red cabbage, carrots, green onions, and celery leaves. Toss with ½ cup of slaw dressing. Season with salt and pepper.

INGREDIENTS:

FOR THE SLAW:

½ cup green cabbage, shaved

½ cup red cabbage, shaved

¼ cup carrots, julienned

1 tablespoon green onions, green part only, thinly sliced

1 tablespoon celery leaves, thinly sliced

1 teaspoon salt

½ teaspoon pepper

FOR THE SLAW DRESSING:

½ cup low-fat Greek yogurt

¼ cup mayonnaise

1 tablespoon rice vinegar

½ tablespoon lime juice

1 teaspoon lime zest

½ teaspoon minced garlic

2 teaspoons Dijon mustard

2 teaspoons salt

JÍCAMA SLAW

INGREDIENTS:

MAKE THE SLAW:

2 cups jícama, peeled and julienned

½ cup green cabbage

½ cup red onion, thinly sliced

¼ cup green apple, julienned

1 whole jalapeño, seeded and julienned

¼ cup cilantro, finely chopped

¼ cup parsley, finely chopped

FOR DRESSING:

2 tablespoons lemon juice

½ tablespoon honey

1½ teaspoons kosher salt

½ teaspoon fresh black pepper

3 tablespoons extra-virgin olive oil

MAKE DRESSING:

In a small bowl, combine lemon juice, honey, salt, and pepper. Whisk together, slowly pouring in the olive oil to emulsify dressing.

MAKE THE SLAW:

In a medium-size bowl, combine all ingredients. Pour dressing over jícama and toss well.

KALE SLAW

MAKE SLAW DRESSING:

In a medium-size bowl, combine all dressing ingredients and whisk to blend well.

MAKE SLAW:

In a medium-size bowl, toss kale, Napa cabbage, and apples with dressing, salt and pepper.

INGREDIENTS:

FOR THE SLAW:

1 packed cup kale, finely chopped

1 packed cup Napa cabbage, finely chopped

1 cup green apple, julienned

1 teaspoon salt

½ teaspoon pepper

FOR THE SLAW DRESSING:

½ cup low-fat Greek yogurt

¼ cup mayonnaise

1 tablespoon rice vinegar

½ tablespoon lime juice

1 teaspoon lime zest

½ teaspoon minced garlic

2 teaspoons Dijon mustard

2 teaspoons salt

TOTAL TIME: 20 minutes

YIELD: 2 cups

NAPA CABBAGE–POMEGRANATE SLAW

INGREDIENTS:

2 cups Napa cabbage, shaved

1 cup celery stalks, thinly sliced

2 tablespoons red onions, thinly sliced

2 tablespoons green onions, green part only, thinly sliced

½ cup pomegranate seeds

1 tablespoon parsley, finely chopped

1 tablespoon fresh cilantro, finely chopped

1 tablespoon fresh mint, finely chopped

1 teaspoon fresh thyme leaves

3 tablespoons extra-virgin olive oil

juice of 1 whole lemon

1 teaspoon salt

1 teaspoon fresh black pepper

In a medium-size bowl, combine Napa cabbage, celery, red onions, green onions, pomegranate seeds, parsley, cilantro, mint, and thyme. Add olive oil, lemon juice, salt, and pepper. Toss well and serve.

NAPA CABBAGE SLAW

INGREDIENTS:

2 cups Napa cabbage, shaved

1 cup celery stalks, thinly sliced

2 tablespoons red onions, thinly sliced

2 tablespoons green onions, green part only, thinly sliced

1 tablespoon parsley, finely chopped

1 tablespoon fresh cilantro, finely chopped

1 tablespoon fresh mint, finely chopped

1 teaspoon thyme

3 tablespoons extra-virgin olive oil

juice of 1 whole lemon

1 teaspoon salt

1 teaspoon fresh black pepper

In a medium-size bowl, combine Napa cabbage, celery, red onions, green onions, parsley, cilantro, mint, and thyme. Add olive oil, lemon juice, salt, and pepper. Toss well and serve.

TOTAL TIME: 20 minutes
YIELD: 2 cups

GREEN CABBAGE SLAW

MAKE SLAW DRESSING:

In a medium-size bowl, combine all dressing ingredients and mix well.

MAKE SLAW:

In a medium-size bowl, combine green cabbage, green apple, and red onions. Add parsley and cilantro. Toss with ½ cup of slaw dressing. Season slaw with salt and pepper.

INGREDIENTS:

FOR THE SLAW:

1 cup green cabbage, shaved or thinly sliced

½ cup green apple, julienned

1 tablespoon red onions, thinly sliced

1 tablespoon fresh parsley, chopped

1 tablespoon fresh cilantro, chopped

½ cup slaw dressing (see recipe)

1 teaspoon salt

½ teaspoon pepper

FOR THE SLAW DRESSING:

½ cup low-fat Greek yogurt

¼ cup mayonnaise

1 tablespoon rice vinegar

½ tablespoon lime juice

1 teaspoon lime zest

½ teaspoon minced garlic

2 teaspoons Dijon mustard

1 tablespoon honey

2 teaspoons salt

RED CABBAGE SLAW

MAKE THE SLAW DRESSING:

In a medium-size bowl, combine all dressing ingredients and whisk to blend well.

MAKE THE SLAW:

In a medium-size bowl, combine red cabbage, carrots, and red onions. Add parsley and cilantro. Toss with ½ cup of slaw dressing. Season slaw with salt and pepper.

INGREDIENTS:

FOR THE SLAW:

1½ cup red cabbage, shaved or thinly sliced

1 cup carrots, julienned

¼ cup red onions, thinly sliced

1 tablespoon fresh parsley, chopped

1 tablespoon fresh cilantro, chopped

½ cup slaw dressing (see recipe)

1 teaspoon salt

½ teaspoon pepper

FOR THE SLAW DRESSING:

½ cup low-fat Greek yogurt

¼ cup mayonnaise

1 tablespoon rice vinegar

½ tablespoon lime juice

1 teaspoon lime zest

½ teaspoon minced garlic

2 teaspoons Dijon mustard

2 teaspoons salt

TOTAL TIME: 20 minutes

YIELD: 2 cups

INGREDIENTS:

FOR THE SLAW:

2 cups green papaya, peeled, seeded and julienned

1 whole red jalapeño, seeded and julienned

¼ cup green onions, julienned

¼ cup fresh mint, finely chopped

¼ cup fresh cilantro, finely chopped

¼ cup roasted peanuts, crushed

FOR DRESSING:

2 tablespoons lemon juice

2 tablespoons lime juice

1 tablespoon orange juice

½ tablespoon agave nectar

1 teaspoon kosher salt

1 teaspoon sesame oil

3 tablespoons extra-virgin olive oil

SPICY GREEN PAPAYA SLAW

MAKE THE DRESSING:

In a small bowl, combine lemon juice, lime juice, orange juice, agave, and salt. Whisk together and slowly pour in sesame oil and olive oil to emulsify dressing.

MAKE THE SLAW:

In a medium-size bowl, combine green papaya, jalapeño, green onion, mint, and cilantro. Pour dressing over papaya and mix well. Finish with crushed peanuts.

TOTAL TIME: 20 minutes

YIELD: 2 cups

CITRUS CARROT SLAW

MAKE THE DRESSING:

In a small bowl, combine agave, mustard, lemon juice, orange juice, salt, and pepper. Mix until well combined. Slowly add olive oil and whisk until emulsified.

MAKE THE SLAW:

In a medium-size bowl, combine all ingredients. Pour ¼ cup of dressing over slaw and toss well.

INGREDIENTS:

FOR THE SLAW:

2 cups carrots julienned

½ cup green cabbage shaved

zest of 1 whole lime

2 tablespoons fresh cilantro finely chopped

FOR THE DRESSING:

1 tablespoon agave nectar

1 teaspoon Dijon mustard

1 tablespoon lemon juice

¼ cup orange juice

1 teaspoon salt

1 teaspoon pepper

¼ cup extra-virgin olive oil

NEW TACO CLASSICS

THE FILLINGS

CHAPTER 8

CHICKEN & POULTRY

I n so many ways, poultry makes the perfect taco filling. Think of the variety of ways we love our weeknight chicken: roasted, grilled, braised, fried, sautéed.

Poultry is beautifully adaptable: We can make it spicy or rich, crispy or soupy. We can cook it with or without skin—either way yields delicious results. Plus, it loves a good marinade, a flavorful rub, or simply salt and pepper.

In the following recipes, we'll show you just how versatile poultry can be in "New Taco Classics" dishes. We'll pile pulled chicken on tostadas, tuck lemony grilled chicken into soft corn tortillas, offer a royal tamarind-glazed duck, fry some crispy chicken chicharrón to pair with kale slaw and lime-chile crema, pair buttermilk fried chicken with a spicy avocado sauce, and more.

RECIPES

WATERCRESS-CHICKEN-AVOCADO-SALAD-STUFFED AREPAS

PREP TIME: 30 minutes
TOTAL TIME: 35 minutes
YIELD: 6 servings

Cool, creamy chicken and avocado salad finds a splendid home in fresh arepas. The salad pops with flavor, with herbaceous notes from fresh cilantro and a sparkle of lime. Tuck it into a warm arepa, and you've got a soulful bite.

1. In a medium bowl, use a fork to smash 1 avocado, and add lime juice, onions, garlic, cilantro, olive oil, salt, and pepper.
2. Combine ingredients with mayonnaise and mustard. Mix in chicken and the remaining diced avocado.

COMPOSE THE AREPA:

1. Using a sharp knife, split open the still-warm arepa like a pita pocket, making a slit in the top and wiggling a knife into the center to create a pocket.
2. Stuff each arepa with watercress followed by the Chicken Avocado Salad.

INGREDIENTS:

6 Arepas (see recipe pg. 7)

2 cups watercress, chopped

Chicken Avocado Salad (see recipe below)

FOR THE CHICKEN AVOCADO SALAD:

2 whole avocados, diced small, divided

1 tablespoon lime juice

1 tablespoon onions, grated

¼ teaspoon garlic, minced

1 tablespoon fresh cilantro, finely chopped

½ tablespoon extra-virgin olive oil

1 teaspoon kosher salt

½ teaspoon fresh ground black pepper

⅓ cup mayonnaise

½ teaspoon Dijon mustard

2 cups cooked chicken breast, finely shredded

PREP TIME: 30 minutes

TOTAL TIME: 40 minutes

YIELD: 4 servings

GRILLED CHICKEN TACOS

INGREDIENTS:

8 Soft Corn Tortillas (see recipe pg. 23)

4 grilled chicken breasts, cut in ½-inch slices (see recipe below)

Pico de Gallo (see recipe pg. 67)

Cilantro Crema (see recipe pg. 110)

Grilled Avocado (see recipe pg. 289)

½ cup Cotija cheese, crumbled

FOR THE GRILLED CHICKEN BREASTS:

4 chicken breasts

1 teaspoon kosher salt

½ teaspoon ground black pepper

1 tablespoon vegetable oil

These chicken tacos are simple—and simply rewarding. Pair them with grilled avocado slices and crumbled Cotija cheese, and they go from simple to majestic.

Preheat grill over high heat. Season the chicken breasts with salt, pepper, and oil. Cook on each side for 10 minutes. Remove chicken from the grill once it is cooked through. Let chicken breasts rest for 3–5 minutes before slicing.

ASSEMBLE THE TACOS:

Fill the warm corn tortillas with the grilled chicken. Top with the Pico de Gallo, Cilantro Crema, Grilled Avocado slices, and Cotija cheese.

CRISPY BUTTERMILK FRIED CHICKEN WITH SPICY GUASACACA

PREP TIME: 30 minutes

TOTAL TIME: 35 minutes

YIELD: 6 servings

There are good reasons why this fried chicken is a work of art: From its brine to its buttermilk bath to its dip in seasoned flour, this recipe yields chicken that's moist and tender inside and beautifully crispy outside.

INGREDIENTS:

6 Arepas (see recipe pg. 7)

1 Crispy Buttermilk Fried Chicken (see recipe below)

Spicy Guasacaca (see recipe pg. 93)

CRISPY BUTTERMILK FRIED CHICKEN:

2 boneless chicken breasts, skin on

2 boneless chicken thighs, skin on

BRINE:

2 quarts water

½ cup kosher salt

HERB SACHET:

Add the following ingredients to a cheesecloth square and tie it with kitchen string:

1 whole thyme sprig

1 whole rosemary sprig

2 bay leaves

6 whole garlic cloves

4 whole black peppercorns

FOR THE INFUSED BUTTERMILK:

4 cups buttermilk

2 tablespoons hot sauce

FOR THE SEASONED FLOUR:

2 cups self-rising flour

2 cups all-purpose flour

1 teaspoon garlic powder

1 teaspoon onion powder

1 tablespoon chile piquín

1 tablespoon smoked paprika

1 tablespoon ground coriander

2 teaspoons kosher salt

2 teaspoons fresh ground black pepper

FOR EGG BATTER:

6 whole eggs

1 teaspoon ground coriander

FOR FRYING:

vegetable oil

1. In a large stockpot, bring 1 quart of water to a simmer and add salt. Dissolve salt in water and remove from heat.
2. Add salt water to 1 quart of cool water in a plastic container. Place herb sachet in combined water and let cool. Place chicken in brine and refrigerate for 12 hours.
3. In a large glass or plastic container, add buttermilk and hot sauce. Remove chicken from brine and add to buttermilk mixture. Cover and refrigerate for 12 hours.
4. In a large bowl, combine all "seasoned flour" ingredients, using a fork or whisk to blend well.

(recipe continues)

5. In another large bowl, whisk together eggs and ground coriander.
6. One by one, remove chicken pieces from buttermilk, allowing excess to drip off.
7. Toss each chicken piece in flour, then dip into eggs, then toss in flour again. Shake off excess between each step.
8. Heat a large deep skillet or fryer, filled about ⅓ high with oil, to 325F degrees.
9. Fry chicken, a few pieces at a time, until golden brown, 8–10 minutes. For extra-crispy consistency, preheat oven to 250F degrees and cook chicken for an additional 5 minutes.

ASSEMBLE THE AREPA:
1. Using a sharp knife, split open the still-warm arepa like a pita pocket, making a slit in the top and wiggling a knife into the center of the arepa to create a pocket.
2. Stuff with the fried chicken and finish with a drizzle of the Spicy Guasacaca on top.

PREP TIME: 20 minutes
TOTAL TIME: 30 minutes
YIELD: 4 servings

QUINOA AND PULLED CHICKEN TOSTADA

These tostadas are piled high with flavor, one healthy layer after another. Shredded chicken and quinoa compose the foundation for a knockout salad that includes pecans, cranberries, and tomatoes tossed in a zesty mustard-agave dressing. The crowning touches: lemony avocado slices and a dollop of Lemon Crema.

INGREDIENTS:

8 Tostadas (see recipe pg. 25)

Quinoa Chicken Salad (see recipe below)

Lemon Crema (see recipe pg. 105)

prepared avocado slices (see instructions below)

FOR THE QUINOA CHICKEN SALAD:

2 cups quinoa, cooked

2 cups cooked chicken, shredded

3 tablespoons, pecans, chopped

¼ cup dried cranberries

1 cup cherry tomatoes, halved

1 cup raw spinach, thinly sliced

¼ cup scallions, thinly sliced

½ cup fresh cilantro leaves

FOR DRESSING:

¼ cup extra-virgin olive oil

1 teaspoon Dijon mustard

1 tablespoon agave syrup

3 tablespoons fresh lemon juice

1½ teaspoons kosher salt

1 teaspoon fresh black pepper

FOR PREPARED AVOCADO:

1 avocado, sliced

⅛ teaspoon crushed red pepper

1 tablespoon lemon juice

MAKE DRESSING:

In a medium-size bowl, combine extra-virgin olive oil, Dijon mustard, agave, lemon juice, salt, and black pepper. Whisk until well combined.

MAKE QUINOA-CHICKEN MIX:

1. In a separate bowl, combine the quinoa, chicken, pecans, cranberries, and tomatoes. Toss until well combined. Add spinach and scallions, and toss again.
2. Add quinoa-chicken-spinach mixture to dressing bowl. Add cilantro. Toss until ingredients are well coated with the dressing.

(recipe continues)

PREPARE THE AVOCADO:

Sprinkle the avocado slices with crushed red pepper and drizzle with 1 tablespoon lemon juice to keep the slices bright in color.

BUILD THE TOSTADAS:

Top the Tostadas with the chicken-quinoa mixture. Drizzle with Lemon Crema and top with the prepared avocado slices.

PREP TIME: 25 minutes

TOTAL TIME: 30 minutes

YIELD: 4 servings

CHICHARRÓN DE POLLO WITH KALE SLAW AND CHILE-LIME CREMA

INGREDIENTS:

8 Cilantro Telitas (See recipe pg. 12)

Kale Slaw (see recipe pg. 121)

Chicharrón de Pollo (see recipe below)

Chile-Lime Crema (see recipe pg. 110)

CHICHARRÓN DE POLLO:

2 boneless chicken breasts, with skin on, cut into 2-inch chunks

2 boneless chicken thighs, with skin on, cut into 2-inch chunks

1 lime, cut in half

1 tablespoon vegetable oil

1 tablespoon Worcestershire sauce

½ cup onion, grated

6 whole garlic cloves, minced

2 teaspoons kosher salt

1 teaspoon fresh ground black pepper

FOR FRYING:

Vegetable oil

BRUSHING LIQUID:

Make a brushing liquid by combining the following ingredients:

2 tablespoons distilled white vinegar

2 tablespoons garlic, minced

2 tablespoons water

There's fried chicken; then there's chicharrón de pollo. What's the difference? A good chicken chicharrón nugget, gifted with supremely crisp skin, is first rubbed with lime. After frying, it's brushed with a garlicky vinegar for a great pop of acidity.

1. Rub all chicken pieces with lime halves. Rinse in cool water and pat dry with paper towels.
2. In a medium-size bowl, stir together vegetable oil, Worcestershire sauce, onion, garlic, salt, and pepper.
3. Add chicken to bowl and coat pieces evenly. Let chicken marinate for 1 hour, covered, in the refrigerator.
4. Remove chicken bowl from refrigerator and let it sit for 20 minutes before frying.
5. Fill a large, deep skillet or fryer ⅓ of the way with vegetable oil and heat to 325F degrees.
6. Fry chicken, a few pieces at a time, until golden brown, about 12–15 minutes.
7. Remove chicken from oil with a slotted spoon, place on a rack, and immediately brush fried chicken with vinegar-water brushing mixture.

ASSEMBLE THE TELITA:

Top the Cilantro Telita with kale slaw, then the Chicharrón de Pollo. Finish with a dollop of the Chile-Lime Crema.

PREP TIME: 25 minutes

TOTAL TIME: 30 minutes

YIELD: Serves 4

SPICED CHICKEN TACOS

A spicy, custom blend of seasonings revs up these ground chicken tacos. The shell, a delicious Cheese Telita, adds a layer of decadence, the red cabbage slaw adds crunch, and the Lime Crema offers a bright note.

INGREDIENTS:

8 Cheese Telitas (see recipe pg. 9)

Ground Chicken (see recipe below)

1 cup red cabbage, shredded

Avocado Croutons (see recipe pg. 335)

Lime Crema (see recipe pg. 106)

FOR THE GROUND CHICKEN:

¼ cup vegetable oil

1 cup onion, chopped

4 whole garlic cloves, minced

¼ cup chile cachucha (sweet chile), chopped

1 pound ground chicken

¾ cup chicken stock

TACO SPICE BLEND:

Make Taco Spice Blend by whisking together the following ingredients:

½ teaspoon garlic powder

½ teaspoon onion powder

1½ tablespoons chili powder

2 teaspoons cornstarch

1 tablespoon ground cumin

2 teaspoons kosher salt

1 teaspoon paprika

1 teaspoon ground coriander

½ teaspoon chile piquín powder

1. In a medium-size skillet, heat vegetable oil at medium-high heat.
2. Add onions to hot oil and cook for 3 minutes, until translucent. Add garlic and cook for an additional minute. Add sweet chiles and sauté for 1 minute.
3. Add ground chicken to skillet, stirring constantly to prevent chicken from clumping. Evenly brown the chicken and cook for 5 minutes.
4. Add Taco Spice Blend and stir well. Once Taco Spice Blend is thoroughly mixed with the chicken, pour chicken stock into the skillet. Cook until liquid reduces, about 4 minutes. Set aside.

ASSEMBLE THE CHEESE TELITAS:

Top the Cheese Telitas with the ground chicken, shredded red cabbage, and Avocado Croutons. Finish with a drizzle of Lime Crema.

PREP TIME: 15 minutes

TOTAL TIME: 35 minutes

YIELD: 4 servings

MANGO CHICKEN TOSTONES

Here's a dish with Caribbean soul: crispy, mango-glazed chicken bites that sit atop a tostón. A classic slaw and Pineapple Pico de Gallo completes the island vibe.

INGREDIENTS:

Tostones (see recipe pg. 315)

Classic Coleslaw (see recipe pg. 117)

Mango chicken (see recipe below)

Pineapple Pico de Gallo (see recipe pg. 81)

flat-leaf parsley sprigs, to garnish

MANGO CHICKEN

4 chicken thighs, boneless and skinless, cut into 1-inch cubes

BUTTERMILK MARINADE

Combine the following ingredients:

1 tablespoon garlic, minced

½ tablespoon fresh rosemary, chopped

½ tablespoon fresh oregano, chopped

½ tablespoon fresh mint, chopped

3 tablespoons buttermilk

1 cup white wine

1½ tablespoons kosher salt

2 tablespoons Worcestershire sauce

½ tablespoon mustard

1 tablespoon orange zest

FOR COOKING:

2 tablespoons olive oil

1 tablespoon brown sugar

1½ cups mango juice

1. In a nonreactive bowl (see explanation on page 65), add chicken and buttermilk marinade. Let the chicken sit in the marinade, covered in the refrigerator, for at least 3 hours, or overnight.
2. Remove chicken from marinade, reserving liquid.
3. Add the olive oil to a large sauté pan over medium heat. Sprinkle in the brown sugar.
4. Sear the chicken on all sides until browned. Add the reserved marinade and cook for 20 minutes.
5. Add the mango juice and cook for another 15 minutes, until the sauce thickens.

BUILD THE TOSTONES:

Top the Tostones with the Classic Coleslaw, followed by the Mango Chicken and Pineapple Pico de Gallo. Garnish each tostón with a sprig of flat leaf parsley on top.

GRILLED MEYER LEMON CHICKEN ON SOFT CORN TORTILLAS

PREP TIME: 30 minutes
TOTAL TIME: 45 minutes
YIELD: 4–6 servings

Macerated Meyer lemons, which keep in the fridge for three weeks, give this grilled chicken its unbelievable flavor. The lemons are pounded with garlic and thyme, then rubbed on the chicken pieces before they hit the grill. The delicious final result is worth the extra steps and maceration time.

MACERATE THE LEMONS (THE DAY BEFORE):

1. Wash lemons in warm water and dry well.
2. Juice 5 of them, quarter the other 5.
3. To a bowl add quartered lemons, salt, sugar, bay leaves, cinnamon sticks, and peppercorns. Toss until combined.
4. Stuff lemons into sterilized jars, packing them tightly to fit as many as possible. Cover with the lemon juice.
5. Wipe jar, screw lid tightly. Place in the refrigerator. The lemons will keep for up to 3 weeks.

GRILL THE MEYER LEMON CHICKEN:

1. Place lemons, garlic, and thyme in a molcajete (or mortar and pestle) and grind them together.
2. Halve the chicken and remove the rib.
3. Rub the lemon-garlic mixture generously on the chicken and under the chicken skin.
4. Season both sides of chicken with a generous amount of salt and fresh black pepper.
5. Place seasoned chicken in a zipped plastic bag with a drizzle of extra-virgin olive oil. Refrigerate overnight.
6. Cut marinated chicken in quarter-inch slices. Grill the chicken over high heat for 10 to 12 minutes, until it's cooked all the way through.

INGREDIENTS:

8–10 Soft Corn Tortillas (see recipe pg. 23)

Grilled Meyer Lemon Chicken (recipe follows)

Napa Cabbage Slaw (see recipe pg. 124)

Citrus Crema (see recipe pg. 105)

Spicy Mango Sauce (see recipe pg. 59)

FOR THE MACERATED MEYER LEMONS:

10 Meyer lemons

½ cup kosher salt

¼ cup sugar

2 bay leaves

2 cinnamon sticks

1 teaspoon black peppercorns

FOR THE GRILLED MEYER LEMON CHICKEN:

1½ cup macerated Meyer lemons

¼ cup garlic, minced

⅓ cup (packed) thyme, stems removed

1 whole organic chicken

kosher salt

freshly ground black pepper

drizzle of extra-virgin olive oil

(recipe continues)

BUILD THE DISH:

1. Warm the tortillas on the hot grill for a few seconds or in the microwave with a damp towel for a few seconds.

2. Top the tortillas with Napa Cabbage Slaw and the grilled chicken. Finish with a dollop of the Citrus Crema on top. Serve with a side of Spicy Mango Sauce.

CHICKEN CHURRASCO TACOS

I love to transform skin-on chicken thighs into flavorful, churrasco-style slices by marinating them in garlic and herbs like oregano, cilantro, rosemary, and mint. Cumin and coriander deepen the flavors while lemon juice and zest give lovely acidity to the chicken. (See image on page xii.)

1. In a molcajete (or mortar and pestle), place garlic, onion, oregano, rosemary, mint, cilantro, jalapeño, ½ teaspoon of the salt, and 1 tablespoon of olive oil. Work until it becomes a paste.

2. Add lemon zest and lemon juice. Combine and transfer to a medium bowl.

3. Add remaining olive oil, cumin, coriander, remaining salt and black pepper. Add the chicken and toss to coat it evenly with the herb mix. Refrigerate, covered, for at least 2 hours, or overnight.

4. Remove chicken bowl from refrigerator and let sit for about 20 minutes. Meanwhile, heat a grill over medium heat.

5. Season the chicken with salt and pepper and place each piece, skin side down, on the hot grill. Cook for 4 minutes, until golden brown, then flip and allow chicken to cook through, about 8–10 minutes.

6. Remove from grill. Let sit for 5 minutes before cutting into ½-inch slices.

BUILD THE TELITA:

Top the Beet Telita with the Citrus Carrot Slaw, then the Chicken Churrasco slices. Add a dollop of the Coconut Avocado Crema on top. Serve alongside the Spicy Pickled Onions.

PREP TIME: 3 hours if making telitas (20 minutes if using ready-made tortillas)

TOTAL TIME: 3 hours and 15 minutes (45 minutes if using ready-made tortillas)

YIELD: 4 servings

INGREDIENTS:

8 Beet Telitas (see recipe pg. 11; or substitute ready-made tortillas)

Citrus Carrot Slaw (see recipe pg. 131)

Herb-Marinated Chicken Churrasco (see recipe below)

Coconut Avocado Crema (see recipe pg. 104)

Spicy Pickled Onions (see recipe pg. 98)

FOR THE HERB-MARINATED CHICKEN CHURRASCO:

8 whole garlic cloves, minced

1 tablespoon onion, minced

1 tablespoon fresh oregano, finely chopped

1 tablespoon fresh rosemary, finely chopped

1 tablespoon fresh mint, finely chopped

1 tablespoon fresh cilantro, finely chopped

½ tablespoon jalapeño, minced

1½ teaspoons kosher salt, divided

¼ cup olive oil, divided

zest of 1 whole lemon

juice of 1 whole lemon

1 teaspoon ground cumin

1 teaspoon ground coriander

1 teaspoon black pepper

4 boneless chicken thighs, skin on

PREP TIME: 20 minutes

TOTAL TIME: 45 minutes

YIELD: 8 servings

INGREDIENTS:

8 Beet Telitas (see recipe pg. 11)

Tamarind Duck (see recipe below)

Pico Verde (see recipe pg. 78)

Avocado Croutons (make full recipe on pg. 335)

TAMARIND DUCK:

1 cup agave nectar

½ cup tamarind pulp

¼ cup fresh lime juice

6 garlic cloves, roasted

4 yellow peppers, roasted or charred

1 whole ají amarillo, seeded

½ cup chicken stock

2 teaspoons ají amarillo powder

2 teaspoons kosher salt

1 teaspoon black pepper

4 duck breast halves, about 8 ounces each, excess fat trimmed

fresh cilantro leaves, for serving

TAMARIND-GLAZED DUCK WITH PICO VERDE

Tamarind, with its sweet, dark notes, seems custom-made for duck. In this recipe, I infuse a tamarind glaze with garlic and the magic of ají amarillo for bolder flavors. Serving the duck atop a Beet Telita not only enhances the sweet note, it reinforces the beautiful red colors of the dish.

1. In a medium-size saucepan, combine agave nectar, tamarind pulp, lime juice, garlic, yellow peppers, ají amarillo, and chicken stock. Bring to a simmer over medium heat and cook for 15 minutes.
2. Remove from heat and let cool for a few minutes. Transfer ingredients to a food processor.
3. Season with ají amarillo powder, salt, and pepper and process until smooth.
4. Pour tamarind glaze into a bowl, set aside to let cool.
5. Preheat a cast-iron skillet over medium-low heat.
6. Meanwhile, score duck breasts diagonally with a sharp knife to prevent curling. Season them with salt and pepper.
7. Place the duck on the skillet, skin side down, and cook, uncovered, until the skin is nicely browned, about 15 minutes.
8. Once almost all of the fat has rendered and the skin is a deep golden brown, flip the duck over and increase the heat to medium.
9. Brush duck with the tamarind glaze and continue cooking for about 5 minutes for medium rare.
10. Place the duck on a cutting board, brush with more of the glaze and let rest for 5 minutes. Slice duck on a diagonal into ¼-inch-thick slices.

TO BUILD:

Spread a little glaze on each Beet Telita. Top with duck slices, then Pico Verde. Crown each with an Avocado Crouton.

AREPA BURGER WITH AVOCADO FRIES

This burger is so flavorful and light, I predict it will become a go-to meal for chicken lovers. Panko crumbs and Greek yogurt give body to the ground chicken, which is seasoned with aromatics, Dijon mustard, and lime.

For a recipe shortcut, replace the White Hominy Arepas with basic Arepas (page 7).

FOR GRILLING:

1. To a large mixing bowl add the ground chicken, panko, Greek yogurt, garlic salt, onion powder, parsley, salt, black pepper, scallions, Dijon mustard, and lime juice. Mix gently until well combined.

2. Divide chicken mixture into 8 equal-sized balls, placing them on wax paper.

3. Flatten each ball into a patty. making a slight indentation in each center. (This helps patties keep their size while grilling.)

4. Place patties in refrigerator for 10 minutes or until set. (The patties must be stiff when you place them on the grill pan.)

5. Heat a grill pan. Add oil to coat.

6. Place the patties on the pan as it is heating up. (Do not wait until pan is fully hot.)

7. Once they are white halfway up the sides, flip them over with a nonstick spatula.

8. Once flipped, let them cook without moving them around. Watch for the bottom half to whiten upwards as did top half.

TO BUILD:

1. Slice the Arepas in half, as you would a hamburger bun. Spread Chipotle Crema inside the top and bottom halves of arepas.

2. Add pickles slices (if using), lettuce, and tomato. Top with chicken patty. Serve with a side of Avocado Fries.

PREP TIME: 30 minutes if using basic Arepa recipe

TOTAL TIME: 2½ hours; 1 hour if using basic Arepa recipe

YIELD: 4 servings

INGREDIENTS:

4 White Hominy Arepas (see recipe pg. 35)

Chipotle Crema (see recipe pg. 104)

pickle slices (optional)

8 leaves of lettuce, the same size as the arepas

1 large tomato, sliced

Chicken Burgers (see recipe below)

Avocado Fries (see recipe pg. 337)

FOR CHICKEN BURGERS:

1 pound ground chicken

½ cup panko crumbs

¼ cup Greek yogurt

1 teaspoon garlic salt

1 teaspoon onion powder

1 tablespoon parsley, finely chopped

1 teaspoon of kosher salt

½ teaspoon black pepper

2 tablespoons scallions, chopped

1 teaspoon Dijon mustard

1 teaspoon lime juice

4 tablespoons oil

PREP TIME: 15 minutes
TOTAL TIME: 20 minutes
YIELD: 4 servings

GROUND TURKEY TACO

A sturdy butter lettuce leaf becomes a refreshing taco shell for this garlicky ground turkey. A Chayote Jalapeño Slaw adds crunch and heat, while the Cilantro Crema cools the bites.

1. Preheat sauté pan over medium-high heat. Add olive oil, then ground turkey to pan. Cook for 3–4 minutes, stirring constantly to break up the turkey meat.
2. Add garlic flakes, fresh garlic, onion, red pepper flakes, and parsley. Stir in red bell pepper, paprika, and white wine. Cook for another 5 minutes, until wine reduces.
3. Season with salt and continue to stir constantly to break down ground turkey. Turn off heat and add fresh parsley.

ASSEMBLE THE DISH:
1. Spoon about ¼ cup of ground turkey mixture into each butter lettuce cup.
2. Top with Chayote Jalapeño Slaw, Pico de Gallo, and a dollop of Cilantro Crema.

INGREDIENTS:

1 Ground Turkey (see recipe below)

8 butter lettuce leaf "cups"

Chayote Jalapeño Slaw (see recipe pg. 116)

Pico de Gallo (see recipe pg. 67)

Cilantro Crema (see pg. 110)

FOR THE GROUND TURKEY:

2 tablespoons olive oil

1 pound ground turkey

½ tablespoon garlic flakes

1 tablespoon fresh garlic, minced

½ cup onion, diced

½ tablespoon red pepper flakes

½ tablespoon dried parsley flakes

¼ cup red bell peppers, diced small

½ tablespoon paprika

¼ cup white wine

1 teaspoon kosher salt

2 tablespoons fresh parsley, minced

PREP TIME: 40 minutes

TOTAL TIME: 50 minutes

YIELD: 4 servings

GREEN TOMATILLO–PULLED CHICKEN TAMALES

It is no ordinary tomatillo sauce that bathes the pulled chicken in this recipe—the tomatillos are first charred on the grill with green peppers and Serrano peppers. The result is a smoky sauce for the chicken and a delicious topping for tamales.

INGREDIENTS:

4 Sweet Corn Tamales (see recipe pg. 33)

Tomatillo Chicken (recipe below)

1 cup grated queso fresco

Spicy Pickled Onions (see recipe pg. 98)

FOR THE TOMATILLO CHICKEN:

6 tomatillos, husked, washed

1 green pepper

2 Serrano peppers

4 tablespoons olive oil

3 cloves garlic, coarsely chopped

1 small red onion, coarsely chopped

1 cup chopped fresh cilantro

1 lime, juiced

2 tablespoons agave syrup

2½ cups of cooked shredded chicken

1 teaspoon ground coriander

1 teaspoon kosher salt

1 teaspoon fresh black pepper

TO WARM TAMALES:

1 tablespoon of butter

MAKE TOMATILLO CHICKEN:

1. Preheat the grill to high heat. Place tomatillos, green pepper, and Serrano peppers on grill and char all sides.
2. In a medium-size sauté pan, heat 2 tablespoons of olive oil. Add grilled tomatillos, grilled green peppers, grilled Serrano peppers, garlic, and onion. Sauté for 5 minutes.
3. Remove pan from heat and place pan ingredients, plus cilantro, lime juice, and agave, in a blender and blend until smooth.
4. Pour the tomatillo mixture into a large heated sauté pan. As the tomatillo sauce simmers, add chicken, coriander, salt, and pepper. Cook for 10 minutes over low heat.

PREPARE THE TAMALES:

1. Melt butter in a griddle over medium-high heat.
2. Unwrap tamales and place them on the griddle for 20 seconds on each side, to warm.

ASSEMBLE THE DISH:

1. Remove Sweet Corn Tamales from heat and center each on a serving plate. Spoon the green Tomatillo Chicken on top of each tamal.
2. Sprinkle with crumbled queso fresco and Spicy Pickled Onions. Serve immediately.

PREP TIME: 25 minutes
TOTAL TIME: 35 minutes
YIELD: 4 servings

AJÍ DE GALLINA TACOS

Once you learn to make this traditional Peruvian chicken dish, you may add it to your comfort-food favorites. Creamy and delicious, the smothered, shredded chicken makes an exquisite topping for crispy telitas.

1. In a small bowl, place bread and milk and let it sit so the bread can absorb the milk.
2. In a large skillet, heat vegetable oil over medium heat. Add onions and garlic, and sauté for 1 minute.
3. Add scallions and almonds slices and sauté for 5 minutes until vegetables are translucent. Remove from heat and set aside.
4. In a blender, combine chicken stock, onion-almond mixture, soaked bread, queso fresco, ají amarillo, and evaporated milk. Blend until smooth. (If overly thick, add a splash of chicken stock.)
5. Season the chicken with salt and place it in the skillet over medium heat. Pour the blended ají amarillo sauce over the chicken and stir until combined. Simmer until the sauce has thickened and fully coats chicken.

BUILD THE DISH:

Top the crispy Cilantro Telitas with Ají de Gallina. Garnish with a wedge of purple potato and a quarter of hard-boiled egg.

INGREDIENTS:

8 Cilantro Telitas (see recipe pg. 12)

Ají de Gallina

FOR AJÍ DE GALLINA:

2 slices white bread, crust removed

½ cup milk

1 tablespoon vegetable oil

¾ cup yellow onion, diced small

6 garlic cloves, minced

2 scallions, thinly sliced

¼ cup almonds, sliced

¼ cup chicken stock

½ cup queso fresco

1½ tablespoons ají amarillo paste

½ cup evaporated milk

2 cooked chicken breasts, shredded

1 teaspoon kosher salt

FOR SERVING:

2 baby purple potatoes, boiled and quartered

2 hard-boiled eggs, quartered

CHAPTER 9

PORK

The humble pig provides some of the most decadent fillings and toppings a taco has experienced. From pork belly to crispy pancetta to glazed meats, pork adds an incomparable earthy and rustic goodness to a dish.

In this chapter, we'll make aromatic pork "al pastor," glazed pork with a prickly pear 'cue sauce, marinate carnitas in tequila and lime, learn to make jerky out of pork tenderloin, and find a new meaning for the abbreviation BLT.

We'll borrow the flavors of Cuba, Mexico, Brazil, Venezuela, Peru, and other parts of Latin America. But in the end, these pork dishes hum with a mix of influences and accents.

PORK RECIPES

PREP TIME: 30 minutes

TOTAL TIME: 3 hours

YIELD: 4 servings

BRAISED PORK TOSTADAS

This oven-braised pork takes its flavor from mostly mild, sweet and smoky chiles, but it does get a kick from ground chile de arbol. The flavors meld nicely in the braise and play well with a corn-studded Peruvian salsa.

1. Preheat the oven to 325F degrees. In a large bowl, whisk together chili powder, cumin, chile de arbol powder, thyme, and salt. Place pork in bowl and turn to coat evenly with rub.
2. In an oven-safe, deep skillet with cover, heat canola oil over medium-high heat. Add pork to hot skillet and sear until golden brown on all sides.
3. Add garlic, onions, ají dulce, Anaheim (or California) chiles, and poblano chiles and cook for 2 minutes. Add chicken stock and bring to a boil.
4. Cover the pan tightly with lid or aluminum foil and place it in the oven to braise for 2½ hours, or until pork is fork tender.
5. Remove the pork from oven and place in a heat-resistant bowl. Shred pork meat with two forks.

BUILD THE TOSTADA:

Put White Bean Spread on each tostada. Place the Braised Pork on top, then crown with the roasted poblano peppers, and Peruvian Corn Salsa Criolla. Sprinkle with the grated Cotija cheese.

INGREDIENTS:

White Bean Spread (see recipe pg. 42)

8 Tostadas (see recipe pg. 25)

Braised Pork (recipe below)

Poblano peppers, roasted and diced

Peruvian Corn Salsa Criolla (see pg. 100)

Cotija cheese, grated

FOR THE BRAISED PORK:

3 tablespoons chili powder

1 tablespoon cumin

1 tablespoon chile de arbol powder

2 tablespoons fresh thyme, finely chopped

2 tablespoons kosher salt

3 pounds boneless pork shoulder, fat cap removed, cut into 2-inch cubes

2 tablespoons canola oil

6 whole garlic cloves, minced

1 cup onions, diced small

¼ cup ají dulce, diced small

¼ cup Anaheim or California chiles, diced small

¼ cup poblano chiles, diced small

2 cups homemade chicken stock or low-sodium chicken broth

CHILE CACHUCHA–GLAZED PORK BELLY

PREP TIME: 30 minutes

TOTAL TIME: 2 hours and 45 minutes

YIELD: 8 servings

The chile glaze on this pork belly is insanely good. Although it is based on the milder cachucha and California chiles, this glaze is full of flavor. The trick is to baste the pork belly with the agave-sweetened glaze as the meat roasts at low heat.

1. Preheat oven to 280F degrees. Season the pork belly with salt, pepper, and ancho chile powder. Scatter chiles and cayenne pepper in a large roasting pan and place the pork belly on top of the chiles, skin side down. Drizzle ½ cup of agave on top of the pork belly.
2. Dilute the remaining agave by whisking into chicken stock or water. Add agave liquid to the roasting pan. Cover tightly with lid or aluminum foil and roast for 2 hours, basting pork with pan juices every 30 minutes.
3. Turn pork belly over and continue roasting until it is fork tender, about 2 more hours.
4. Transfer pork to a deep tray or plate, reserving the pan juices, and set it aside to cool. Once pork has cooled, cover it with parchment or waxed paper. Place a large plate over the covered pork belly and weigh it down with heavy cans or a foil-wrapped brick. Refrigerate pork this way overnight.
5. Strain the liquid from the roasting pan into a saucepan, reserving the chiles.
6. Simmer the sauce for about 30 to 45 minutes until it is reduced to about 1 cup. Add reserved chiles and remove thickened sauce from the heat. Set aside to let the glaze cool, then place in the refrigerator to chill.
7. When you are ready to serve the dish, remove pork belly from refrigerator. Preheat a large, heavy skillet or cast-iron pan over medium heat.

INGREDIENTS:

8 Cheese Telitas (see recipe pg. 9)

Serrano Pico de Gallo (see recipe pg. 82)

Chile Cachucha–Glazed Pork Belly (recipe follows)

FOR THE CHILE–CACHUCHA PORK BELLY:

3 pounds pork belly, no rib bones

3 teaspoons kosher salt

2 teaspoons freshly ground black pepper

2 teaspoons ancho chile powder

8 cachucha chiles, chopped

2 California chiles, chopped

1 fresh cayenne pepper, chopped

1 cup agave syrup, divided

2 cups chicken stock or water

(recipe continues)

8. Slice pork belly into 1-inch wedges. Sear each side of the pork belly until it's crispy and heated through, about 3 minutes each side. Reheat the glaze and brush it on the pork.

BUILD THE TELITA:
Top the Cheese Telita with the Serrano Pico de Gallo. Crown with a slice of Chile Cachucha–Glazed Pork Belly.

TOSTADAS AL PASTOR

Chipotle and cumin add smoky notes to the pork that's featured in this recipe. A leisurely marinade infuses the meat with the aroma of oregano and chiles, and pineapple adds sweet notes.

1. In a blender, make a marinade by adding half of the chopped onions and half of the chopped pineapple. Add orange juice, half of the garlic, vinegar, chile de arbol, salt, oregano, cumin, chile en adobo, and 3 tablespoons of the chopped cilantro. Blend until smooth.
2. Place pork in a resealable plastic bag, and pour the marinade over it to cover the pork. Seal the bag and turn to coat the meat well. Set bag aside in the refrigerator for at least 4 hours or overnight.
3. In a large skillet, heat vegetable oil over high heat. To the hot oil add remaining onions and pineapple. Add the marinated pork and sear for 6 to 8 minutes on each side, until cooked through.
4. Season the pork with salt and pepper and remove pan from heat. Sprinkle pork with fresh cilantro. Set aside.

BUILD THE TOSTADA:

Cover the Tostadas with the Pinto Bean Spread, then add the Pork al Pastor, fresh cilantro, and onion. Serve with a lime wedge.

PREP TIME: 15 minutes
TOTAL TIME: 25 minutes
YIELD: 6 servings

INGREDIENTS:

12 Tostadas (see recipe pg. 25)

Pinto Bean Spread (see recipe pg. 41)

Pork al Pastor (recipe below)

½ cup cilantro, chopped

½ cup yellow onions, diced

lime wedges

FOR THE PORK AL PASTOR:

1 large white onion, diced small, divided

1 pineapple, peeled, diced small, divided

½ cup fresh orange juice

¼ cup garlic, minced, divided

¼ cup distilled white vinegar

¼ cup chile de arbol powder

2 teaspoons kosher salt

1 teaspoon dried oregano, preferably Mexican

2 teaspoons ground cumin

2 chipotle chiles en adobo

½ cup fresh cilantro, chopped, divided

2½ pounds pork loin, cut into ½-inch cubes

3 tablespoons vegetable oil

freshly ground black pepper, to taste

fresh cilantro, chopped, for sprinkling

PREP TIME: 25 minutes
TOTAL TIME: 35 minutes
YIELD: 4 servings

INGREDIENTS:

8 Soft Corn Tortillas (see recipe pg. 23)

Cuban-Style Pork (recipe follows)

¼ cup cilantro sprigs

lime wedge

FOR THE CUBAN-STYLE PORK:

1 pound pork loin, cut into bite-size cubes

8 whole garlic cloves, minced

1 teaspoon kosher salt

½ teaspoon black pepper

2 teaspoons fresh oregano, finely chopped

1 teaspoon fresh thyme, finely chopped

¼ cup olive oil

¼ cup orange juice

¼ cup lemon juice

zest of 1 whole lemon

zest of 1 orange

2 tablespoons vegetable oil

FOR THE SMOTHERED ONIONS:

2 tablespoons butter

2 cups white onion, thinly sliced

1 tablespoon white wine vinegar

1 tablespoon lime juice

1 tablespoon celery leaves, finely chopped

1 teaspoon kosher salt

1 teaspoon fresh black pepper

CUBAN-STYLE PORK

More than a squeeze of lime or orange, it is the zest of the citrus ingredients in this recipe that gives this pork a great sparkle of flavor. I love working with citrus zest because it adds instant and lasting flavor. Add the pungency of garlic and the sweetness of smothered onions, and the dish takes on a classic Cuban dimension.

MAKE THE PORK:

1. In a 1-gallon resealable plastic bag, place pork loin cubes, garlic, salt, pepper, oregano, thyme, olive oil, orange juice, lemon juice, lemon zest, and orange zest. Set aside and let pork marinate in the refrigerator for at least 2½ hours or overnight.
2. Preheat oven to 350F degrees. Remove pork from refrigerator and remove excess marinade from pork cubes.
3. Heat sauté pan over high heat. Add vegetable oil and pork to the pan. Sauté pork cubes until they are seared, about 2 minutes.
4. Spread browned pork cubes on a rimmed baking sheet and set sauté pan aside for the moment. Place the baking sheet in the hot oven and roast the pork chunks at 350F degrees for 10 minutes.
5. Turn the oven to broil and cook the pork at the higher heat for 5 minutes, until golden brown.

MAKE THE SMOTHERED ONIONS:

1. In the sauté pan, add butter and onions and sauté over medium-high heat for about 2 minutes, until the onions are translucent.
2. Squeeze lime juice over the onions and add vinegar, remove pan from heat. Finish with celery leaves, salt, and pepper.

BUILD THE TACO:

On a warm corn tortilla, place the pork chunks and top with the Smothered Onions. Garnish with a sprig of cilantro and a lime wedge.

PRICKLY PEAR BBQ PORK

PREP TIME: 30 minutes

TOTAL TIME: 4 hours, 30 minutes

YIELD: 6 servings

Prickly pears, which can range in flavor from watermelon-sweet to kiwi-tart, give great character to the sauce in this recipe. Pork loves a little acid and sweetness—and it gets that from this sauce. A word of caution: Prickly pears can be, yes, prickly to handle. My suggestion is to use tongs to hold the fruit with one hand, while you slice off the skin with a knife. (Or use a thick kitchen towel to protect your hands.)

INGREDIENTS:

6 Puffy Tortillas (see recipe pg. 29)

Prickly Pear BBQ Pulled Pork (recipe follows)

Classic Coleslaw (see recipe pg. 117)

Blue Cheese Crema (see recipe pg. 103)

FOR THE PRICKLY PEAR BBQ PULLED PORK:

1½ pounds pork loin

1 teaspoon fresh thyme, chopped

1 teaspoon garlic flakes

1 teaspoon red pepper flakes

2 teaspoons dried parsley

2 teaspoons kosher salt

1 teaspoon fresh black pepper

3 tablespoons lemon juice

3 tablespoons orange juice

3 whole garlic cloves, minced

1 tablespoon olive oil

2 tablespoons vegetable oil, for sautéing

FOR THE PRICKLY PEAR BBQ SAUCE:

4 whole prickly pears, peeled

2 tablespoons unsalted butter

2 celery stalks, finely chopped

2 leeks, white parts only, finely chopped

1 whole onion, diced small

3 whole garlic cloves, minced

1 cup ketchup

1 cup beef stock

¼ cup coconut vinegar

¼ cup Champagne vinegar

2 tablespoons Worcestershire sauce

¼ cup dark rum

¼ cup molasses

½ cup honey

1 teaspoon dry mustard

1 teaspoon ground cumin

1 teaspoon kosher salt

½ teaspoon chile piquín or chili powder

MAKE THE PORK:

1. In a large bowl, place pork loin, thyme, garlic flakes, red pepper flakes, dried parsley, salt, pepper, lemon juice, orange juice, garlic cloves, and olive oil. Cover bowl and set aside in refrigerator to marinate for at least 2½ hours or overnight.

2. Heat a sauté pan over high heat; add vegetable oil to the pan. Remove pork loin from bowl, reserving the marinade. Brown the pork in hot oil evenly on all sides, about 2 minutes on each side.

(recipe continues)

3. Add the marinade to the sauté pan and remove pan from heat.
4. Place pork loin and marinating liquid in a slow cooker.

MAKE THE SAUCE:
1. Blend the prickly pears and strain to remove seeds. (Makes about 1½ cups of pear juice.)
2. In a medium-size saucepan over medium heat, melt butter and add celery, leeks, onions, and garlic and sauté until onions soften.
3. To the saucepan, stir in the prickly pear juice, ketchup, beef stock, coconut vinegar, Champagne vinegar, Worcestershire sauce, dark rum, molasses, honey, dry mustard, ground cumin, salt, and chile piquín. Simmer and stir until sauce is well combined.
4. Take half of this sauce and pour it into the slow cooker with the pork loin. Set slow cooker to high and cook for 4 hours (or use the "pork" setting on your slow cooker).
5. Bring the remaining sauce to a boil. Reduce to a simmer for about 1 hour, or until the sauce is reduced by half.

PULL THE PORK:
1. Using 2 forks or your fingers, pull pork apart into individual bite-size pieces.
2. Add the pulled pork to the sauce and simmer until the meat and sauce are well combined.

BUILD THE TACO:
Place the Puffy Tortillas on the center of a plate. Top with the Prickly Pear BBQ Pork, then the Classic Coleslaw. Finish with a drizzle of the Blue Cheese Crema.

PREP TIME: 45 minutes

TOTAL TIME: 3½ to 4 hours slow-cooked; 35 to 45 minutes in pressure cooker

YIELD: 8 servings

TEQUILA-LIME CARNITAS

These carnitas sit in a spicy-sweet marinade that gives them their flavor foundation. They make a hearty topping for sopes and contrast nicely with the Chayote Slaw. This low-and-slow recipe makes a delicious Sunday lunch or supper, and it's perfect for busy families—set the slow cooker in the morning and your carnitas will be hot and ready when you get home. For best results, the slow-cooked method is best.

INGREDIENTS:

8 Sopes (see recipe pg. 30)

Tequila-Lime Carnitas (recipe follows)

Chayote Jalapeño Slaw (see recipe pg. 116)

Cilantro Crema (see recipe pg. 110)

FOR THE TEQUILA-LIME CARNITAS:

3 pounds boneless pork shoulder, fat cap removed, cut into 2-inch cubes

6 whole garlic cloves, minced

1 cup onions, diced small

½ cup lime juice

zest of 3 limes

½ cup tequila

½ cup orange juice

zest of 1 orange

¼ cup fresh cilantro, finely chopped

¼ cup ají dulce or ají cachucha, diced small

¼ cup Anaheim chiles, chopped

2 tablespoons jalapeño, minced

1 tablespoon ancho chile powder

3 tablespoons honey

½ tablespoon kosher salt

1 teaspoon ground black pepper

2 tablespoons canola oil

2 tablespoons cilantro, finely chopped

1 tablespoon mint, finely chopped

SHORTCUT: If time is an issue, use a pressure cooker instead of a slow cooker to reduce your cooking time by more than half.

1. In a large bowl combine pork, garlic, onion, lime juice, lime zest, tequila, orange juice, orange zest, cilantro, ají dulce, Anaheim chiles, jalapeño, ancho chile powder, honey, salt, and pepper. Marinate at least 2½ hours or overnight in the refrigerator.

(recipe continues)

2. In a large, deep oven-safe skillet with cover, heat canola oil over medium-high heat. Add pork to skillet and sear until golden brown on all sides. Add marinade to skillet and let it cook for 2–3 minutes.

3. Cover the pan tightly with aluminum foil or lid and cook over low heat for 3½ to 4 hours (or transfer ingredients to a slow cooker, set on high), or until pork is fork tender. Remove the pork from pan and place in a heat-resistant bowl. (If using a pressure cooker, add skillet-seared pork to pot and cook for 35 to 45 minutes.)

4. Let sauce cool slightly, then place it in a blender. Blend until smooth and return sauce to skillet. Bring to a boil. (If using an immersion blender, blend sauce in saucepan and bring to a boil.) Let sauce reduce by half, about 15 minutes.

5. Shred pork with two forks. Spoon some of the reduced sauce over the shredded pork and garnish with chopped cilantro and mint.

BUILD THE SOPES:

Top the Sopes with the Tequila Lime Carnitas and then the Chayote Jalapeño Slaw. Finish with a drizzle of Cilantro Crema.

PREP TIME: 20 minutes
TOTAL TIME: 4 hours
YIELD: 4 servings

INGREDIENTS:

tortilla chips (store-bought is fine)

Chipotle Carnitas (recipe below)

2 cups Monterey Jack cheese, shredded

Citrus Crema (see recipe pg. 105)

FOR THE CHIPOTLE CARNITAS:

3 pounds pork shoulder

2 teaspoons kosher salt

1 teaspoon ground black pepper

2 tablespoons vegetable oil

1 whole onion, chopped

1 teaspoon cumin

1 teaspoon smoked paprika

6 whole garlic cloves, chopped

3 whole chipotle peppers, chopped

14 ounces canned tomatoes, with liquid, diced

2 tablespoons adobo sauce

1 whole bay leaf

1 teaspoon dried oregano

3 cloves

½ cup beef stock or water

CHIPOTLE CARNITAS NACHOS

The smoky notes of chipotle and paprika infuse these carnitas, which make a delicious and unexpected topping for nachos. Beneath a bubbling layer of melted Jack cheese, they smolder with flavor. Add a dollop of Citrus Crema for cool contrast.

1. Season pork shoulder with salt and pepper. In a Dutch oven or roaster, heat oil over medium-high heat. Sear the pork until golden brown, making sure that all sides are nicely seared. Remove the pork from pot and set aside.
2. Add the onion to pot and sauté until lightly browned. Add cumin, paprika, garlic, and chopped chipotle and sauté for about 30 seconds.
3. Stir in the tomatoes with their liquid, the adobo sauce, bay leaf, dried oregano, cloves, and stock or water, making sure to scrape the bottom of the pan.
4. Return pork to the pan, bring ingredients to a boil, then lower heat to a simmer. Braise the pork until the meat falls apart, about 3–4 hours (about 6 hours in a slow cooker).
5. Remove the pork and set aside. Remove cloves and bay leaf from braising liquid. Place braising liquid in a food processor or a blender and puree into a sauce. Simmer the sauce on the stovetop for about 3–5 minutes.
6. Using two forks, shred the pork shoulder. Return the shredded meat to the simmering sauce and let it soak up the flavor and juices and heat through. Set aside.

BUILD THE NACHOS:

1. Preheat the oven to 350F degrees. Arrange the tortilla chips on an ovenproof platter and top them with the Chipotle Carnitas and grated Monterey cheese.
2. Place in the oven for 10 minutes to melt the cheese. Remove platter from oven. Serve Nachos with dollops of Citrus Crema on top or on the side.

PREP TIME: 25 minutes
TOTAL TIME: 35 minutes
YIELD: 4–6 servings

SAUSAGE AND PEPPERS

My take on a traditional sausage-and-peppers combo starts with a good amount of cured pork linguiça sausage. This smoke-cured, mildly spicy sausage, typically sold in longish links, is popular in Brazil and other places rich in Brazilian or Portuguese heritage. It's longer and thinner than your typical chorizo, so it requires less cooking time than chorizo or thicker sausages. Linguiça is delicious with a colorful mix of bell peppers.

1. Prepare a hot charcoal or gas grill. Season linguiça sausage liberally on both sides with salt and pepper. Place sausage on hot grill and cook without moving until there are grill marks, 4–5 minutes. Turn sausage over and cook another 4–5 minutes. Remove sausage from grill and cut into 2-inch slices.

2. In a large skillet, heat oil over medium-high heat. Sauté onions, garlic and all the peppers for about 2 minutes. Add linguiça and sauté for another minute or 2. Remove from heat, sprinkle with fresh cilantro, and set aside.

TO BUILD:

Warm the flour tortillas on the grill for about 20 seconds. Serve the Sausage and Peppers on a platter with a side of Spicy Guasacaca. Serve the warm tortillas on the side.

INGREDIENTS:

6 flour tortillas, warm

Linguiça Sausage and Peppers (recipe below)

Spicy Guasacaca (see recipe pg. 93)

FOR THE LINGUIÇA SAUSAGE AND PEPPERS:

1 pound linguiça sausage (or other smoky pork sausage)

kosher salt

freshly ground black pepper

2 tablespoons vegetable oil

¼ cup onions, thinly sliced

3 garlic cloves, minced

¼ cup green peppers into strips

¼ cup yellow peppers into strips

¼ cup red peppers into strips

2 tablespoons fresh cilantro, chopped

PREP TIME: 20 minutes

TOTAL TIME: 25 minutes

YIELD: 4 servings

INGREDIENTS:

Pork Tenderloin Jerky
(recipe below)

Jícama Slaw (see recipe
pg. 118)

radishes, thinly sliced

½ cup cilantro leaves

8 Cheese Telitas (see recipe
pg. 9)

FOR THE PORK TENDERLOIN JERKY:

3 tablespoons sugar

2 garlic cloves, minced

2 lemongrass, finely
chopped

½ tablespoon ají amarillo

1 tablespoon fresh ginger,
grated

½ cup soy sauce

3 tablespoons olive oil

2 tablespoons vegetable oil

1 tablespoon sesame oil

1 pound pork tenderloin,
thinly sliced

PORK TENDERLOIN JERKY

My version of pork jerky doesn't require dehydrating the meat, but it does call for a bold mix of Asian-meets-Peruvian flavor notes.

1. In a mixing bowl, put together all ingredients, except for the pork and whisk until well combined.
2. Add the pork slices to the marinade and cover bowl with plastic wrap. Set aside in the refrigerator to marinate for at least 2 hours or overnight.
3. Remove pork from refrigerator. Heat a grill or skillet on stovetop over medium heat. Remove the pork from the marinade (discard marinade), and sear the meat for 1 to 1½ minutes per side. Turn off the heat and set aside.

TO BUILD:

On a serving platter, arrange the jerky slices in a fanned-out pattern. Top with Jícama Slaw and garnish with radishes and cilantro. Serve with a side of Cheese Telitas.

BRAISED PORK PLANTAIN LEAF TAMAL

PREP TIME: 30 minutes

TOTAL TIME: 40–45 minutes

YIELD: 12 servings

This tamal masa is made heartier by a heap of Braised Pork. Steamed together, they create a full meal in a simple plantain leaf.

MAKE ACHIOTE OIL:

Warm a saucepan over medium heat and add oil. When oil is hot, add the achiote seeds and turn off the heat. Let pan sit until it cools. Strain the oil for use in tamal recipe.

MAKE THE TAMALES:

1. In a large mixing bowl, combine corn flour, chicken stock, Braised Pork, and Achiote Oil. Mix with hands until ingredients are well combined. Let the masa mixture sit for a few minutes.
2. Place a plantain leaf on a flat surface. Add approximately 3 tablespoons of the masa mixture, spreading the dough with the belly of the spoon to create a rectangle that's approximately 5½ inches by 3 inches in size.
3. Fold the leaf in half, and then fold the fully open edge to secure the filling.
4. Fold the ends of the leaf toward the center, creating a perfect folded rectangle.
5. Drape a second plantain leaf, 3 inches by 8 inches, around the tamal to secure it into a rectangle.
6. Tie each tamal with butcher's string, to secure.
7. Place the tamales in a steamer for 35 to 40 minutes. Remove tamales and place on a tray. Allow them to sit for 5 minutes before serving.
8. Garnish with Salsa Criolla and serve with a side of Spicy Rocoto Sauce.

INGREDIENTS:

1 cup precooked corn flour

1 cup of chicken stock

2 cups of Braised Pork (see recipe on page 168, Braised Pork Tostadas recipe)

2 tablespoons of Achiote Oil (recipe below)

Salsa Criolla (see recipe pg. 99)

Spicy Rocoto Sauce (see recipe pg. 63)

FOR WRAPPING TAMALES:

plantain leaves, 8 inches by 10 inches each (frozen banana leaves can be used)

butcher's string, for tying

FOR ACHIOTE OIL:

1 cup of vegetable oil

2 tablespoons of achiote (annatto) seeds

PREP TIME: 10 minutes

COOK TIME: 15 minutes

TOTAL TIME: 25

YIELD: 4 servings

INGREDIENTS:

4 thin slices pancetta

1 yellow tomato, sliced into at least four ½-inch rounds

1 red tomato, sliced into at least four ½-inch rounds

2 tablespoons olive oil

1 tablespoon balsamic vinegar

kosher salt

black pepper

8 fried cheese slices (queso para freír), ¼-inch wedges

4 Cheese Telitas (see recipe pg. 9)

1 cup spinach

4 fried eggs

CRISPY PANCETTA, ROASTED TOMATO, AND CHEESE TELITAS

This dish is what you might get if you were to cross a BLT with a taco. But instead of traditional bacon slices, I use crispy pancetta. I replace the lettuce with spinach, add a wedge of fried cheese and a fried egg—because in this book, BLT stands for Bold Latin Taco.

1. Preheat oven to 350F degrees. On a rack with a drainage tray, place pancetta in the oven for 15 minutes.
2. Arrange tomato slices on a rimmed baking sheet. Season them with olive oil, balsamic vinegar, salt, and pepper. Roast tomatoes in the oven for 15 minutes.
3. In a nonstick, medium-size skillet over medium heat, fry the cheese for 30 seconds per side.

BUILD THE TELITAS:

Top each of the Cheese Telitas with 5 leaves of spinach, then a slice of pancetta. Add slices of yellow and red tomatoes. Crown each Telita with a fried egg and fried cheese slices.

CHAPTER 10

FISH & SEAFOOD

A fresh fish taco is one of my favorite meals. I love the simplicity of it, the way the flavor of the fresh-caught fish is enhanced on the grill or in the fryer. I love the contrast of toppings. And I love that the dish is easy to make.

The waters surrounding and flowing throughout Latin America offer some of the most stellar fillings for our tacos. Anyone who has taken a bite of a flavorful fish taco knows this well. In the recipes that follow, we'll explore beyond the classic fish taco and swim into exciting new waters. We'll top tostadas with fresh ceviche, create taco fillings of spicy tuna and tuna tartare, whip up some spicy, crackling calamari, pair smoked salmon and sweet potato arepas, and much more.

Whether they're grilled, fried, sautéed, or raw, fish and seafood offer us a world of possibilities when it comes to fillings and toppings. And the beauty of these fillings is that many times they are as delicious raw as they are cooked.

RECIPES

TEMPURA JUMBO SHRIMP

PREP TIME: 30 minutes

TOTAL TIME: 35 minutes

YIELD: 8 servings

These tacos are all about flavor and textural contrasts: The shrimp's crispy and super-light tempura coat contrasts with the soft but sturdy blue corn tortillas. A spicy onion-jalapeño topping contrasts with a sweet and smoky peach-chipotle sauce. To achieve an airy crunch factor, cornstarch and seltzer are added to the tempura batter.

INGREDIENTS:

Onion-jalapeño topping (see recipe below)

8 Blue Corn Tortillas (see recipe pg. 26)

Tempura Jumbo Shrimp (recipe below)

Spicy Peach Chipotle Sauce (see recipe pg. 59)

FOR THE TEMPURA JUMBO SHRIMP:

vegetable oil, for frying

⅔ cup all-purpose flour

¼ cup cornstarch

1 teaspoon fresh thyme, finely chopped

1 tablespoon fresh cilantro, finely chopped

1 tablespoon fresh mint, finely chopped

1 teaspoon ancho chile powder

1½ cups cold seltzer water

8 jumbo shrimp, tail on, cleaned and deveined

FOR THE ONION-JALAPEÑO TOPPING:

½ cup red onions, thinly sliced

1 jalapeño, thinly sliced

¼ cup cilantro, chopped

½ tablespoon olive oil

kosher salt

black pepper

MAKE THE TEMPURA JUMBO SHRIMP:

1. In a large deep skillet or fryer, heat oil to 350F degrees.
2. In a cold, large bowl, whisk together flour, cornstarch, thyme, cilantro, mint, and ancho chile powder. Slowly whisk in seltzer water, being careful not to overmix. (This step is the key to keeping the batter light.)
3. Dip shrimp into tempura batter, coating evenly. Fry immediately by carefully dropping shrimp into fryer. Cook for 1–2 minutes.
4. Once shrimp floats to the top, remove each with a slotted spoon and place on a rack to drain. Season with salt.

MAKE ONION-JALAPEÑO TOPPING:

In a small bowl, mix the red onions, jalapeño, cilantro, olive oil, salt and pepper.

TO BUILD:

Place onion-jalapeño relish on top of the Blue Corn Tortillas, then top each with 1 Tempura Jumbo Shrimp. Serve with a side of Spicy Peach Chipotle Sauce.

PREP TIME: 20 minutes

TOTAL TIME: 25 minutes

YIELD: 4 servings

CEVICHE TOSTADAS

CEVICHE, SWEET POTATO MASH, AND CORN SALAD

Fresh ceviche is a no-cook dish that can be enjoyed throughout the year. During summer, the bright, fresh citrus flavors of a good ceviche are perfect for steamy days, and when paired with a clove-infused sweet potato mash, the dish takes on beautiful fall and winter notes. The trick in making this recipe is to keep the fish and leche de tigre very cold.

INGREDIENTS:

FOR THE CORN SALAD:

¼ cup red onion, very thinly sliced

½ red jalapeño, thinly sliced

½ cup lemon juice

1½ teaspoons kosher salt, divided

2½ tablespoon fresh cilantro, finely chopped, divided

½ cup Peruvian corn (choclo)

FOR THE CEVICHE:

½ teaspoon rocoto paste

1 pound hogfish or red snapper, cut into ¼-inch cubes (reserve 2–3 cubes for leche de tigre)

¼ cup red onion, finely chopped

½ red jalapeño, finely chopped

1 whole large sweet potato, boiled, mashed, seasoned with salt*

FOR THE LECHE DE TIGRE:

¼ cup white onions, roughly chopped

½ celery stalk, roughly chopped

¼ teaspoon garlic, minced

⅓ cup lime juice

¼ cup lemon juice

2–3 pieces of the reserved fish **

½ cup fish stock

1 cup ice

½ tablespoon kosher salt

⅛ teaspoon ají amarillo

½ tablespoon fresh cilantro, roughly chopped

1 teaspoon ginger, peeled and grated

12 round wonton wrappers, fried

MAKE THE LECHE DE TIGRE:

In a blender, add onions, celery stalk, garlic, lime juice, lemon juice, fish, fish stock, ice, salt, ají amarillo, cilantro, and ginger. Blend until smooth, strain, and place in refrigerator. It should always be kept cold until used.

---

* To add hints of baking spices to the sweet potato, boil it in 2 cups water, 3 tablespoons sugar, 2 cloves, and 1 cinnamon stick. When tender, mash the potato.

** When making leche de tigre, add to the blender 2–3 pieces of the same fish you are using in the ceviche. It creates a thicker consistency without using cream.

(recipe continues)

MAKE THE CORN SALAD:

In a medium bowl, combine thinly sliced red onions, thinly sliced red jalapeño, lemon juice, ½ teaspoon salt, ½ tablespoon cilantro, and Peruvian corn. Let marinate for 20 minutes on countertop.

MAKE THE CEVICHE:

1. Coat the bottom of a large bowl with ½ teaspoon of rocoto paste.
2. Add fish, chopped red onions, chopped red jalapeño, 2 tablespoons cilantro, and ½ teaspoon of salt.
3. Add leche de tigre to fish and let sit for 5 minutes in the refrigerator.

MAKE THE TOSTADA:

1. Fry wonton wrappers until golden brown and season with salt.
2. With a spoon, spread 1 tablespoon of sweet potato mash on a fried wonton. Place 1 to 1½ tablespoons of ceviche on top of sweet potato. Top with sliced onion, jalapeño, and corn salad.

SPICY TUNA

This bite is as beautiful to the eye as it is to the palate: A vibrantly red Beet Reinita is topped with fresh, raw tuna. The spicy elements of the marinated fish contrast nicely with the earthy reinita.

In a cold, medium-sized bowl, mix together tuna, red jalapeño, red onions, parsley, lemon zest, extra-virgin olive oil, red pepper flakes, salt, and pepper.

TO BUILD:

Place the spicy tuna on top of the Beet Reinita and top with the fresh avocado.

INGREDIENTS:

12 Beet Reinitas (see recipe pg. 18)

Spicy Tuna (recipe below)

1 avocado, cut into small cubes

FOR THE SPICY TUNA:

8 ounces fresh tuna, cut into small cubes

2 tablespoons red jalapeño, diced small

2 tablespoons red onions, diced small

2 tablespoons fresh parsley, finely chopped

½ teaspoon lemon zest

1 tablespoon extra-virgin olive oil

pinch of red pepper flakes

2 teaspoons kosher salt

pinch fresh ground black pepper

PREP TIME: 15 minutes
TOTAL TIME: 20 minutes
YIELD: 4 servings

TUNA TARTARE

A touch of sushi caviar lends salty notes to this delicious tartare made of sushi-grade raw tuna. A tostada base and crispy shallots add crunch to the combo.

In a cold, medium-sized bowl, mix together tuna, caviar, red onion, cilantro, salt and olive oil.

TO BUILD:
Top tostadas with Tuna Tartare and Red Cabbage Slaw and finish with Crispy Shallots.

INGREDIENTS:

8 Tostadas (see recipe pg. 25)

Tuna Tartare (see recipe below)

Red Cabbage Slaw (see recipe pg. 127)

Crispy Shallots (see recipe pg. 340)

FOR THE TUNA TARTARE:

8 ounces fresh tuna, deveined and finely chopped

1 tablespoon sushi caviar

1 tablespoon red onion, diced small

1 tablespoon fresh cilantro, finely chopped

1 teaspoon kosher salt

1 tablespoon extra-virgin olive oil

PREP TIME: 20 minutes

TOTAL TIME: 25 minutes

YIELD: 4 servings

CRUNCHY FISH STICKS

Hello, New World fish sticks! These crispy fried sticks offer hints of cumin, cilantro, and Peruvian ají amarillo.

1. In a medium-sized bowl, whisk together egg, milk, and water. Add cumin, ají amarillo, oregano, cilantro, baking powder, and salt.
2. Place precooked cornmeal in a separate medium bowl.
3. Dip each fish stick into egg mixture and shake off excess. Then coat in precooked cornmeal, pressing lightly to ensure crumbs stick to fish.
4. Carefully drop fish into fryer. Cook for 1½ to 2 minutes. Remove each fish stick from hot oil with a slotted spoon and place on a rack to drain. Season with salt immediately.

TO BUILD:

Warm the tortillas on the hot grill for a few seconds or in the microwave with a damp towel for a few seonds. Top with the Napa Cabbage Slaw, Battered Fish sticks, and Chipotle Crema. Serve with Pico de Gallo on the side.

INGREDIENTS:

8 Soft Corn Tortillas (see recipe pg. 23)

Napa Cabbage Slaw (see recipe pg. 124)

Battered Fish (see recipe below)

Chipotle Crema (see recipe pg. 104)

Pico de Gallo (see recipe pg. 67)

FOR THE BATTERED FISH:

1 whole egg

½ cup milk

½ cup water

1 teaspoon ground cumin

¼ teaspoon ají amarillo

½ teaspoon ground oregano

1 tablespoon fresh cilantro, finely chopped

1 teaspoon baking powder

1 teaspoon kosher salt

1 cup precooked white cornmeal

1 pound fresh firm white fish (tilapia, grouper, snapper), cut into 4-inch-by-1-inch sticks

PREP TIME: 15 minutes

TOTAL TIME: 25 minutes

YIELD: 4 servings

FISH AND CHIPS

INGREDIENTS:

Battered Fish (see recipe pg. 203)

Avocado Fries (recipe pg. 337)

Chipotle Crema (see recipe pg. 104)

Seasoned Lemon and Limes (see recipe pg. 332)

My Fish and Chips speak with a Latin American accent, from the cumin in the fish batter to the Chipotle Crema sauce on the side. And the chips? They're Avocado Fries.

TO BUILD:

Serve the Battered Fish Sticks and Avocado Fries side by side with a serving of the Chipotle Crema for dipping. Complete the combo with Seasoned Lemons and Limes.

PREP TIME: 15 minutes

TOTAL TIME: 20 minutes

YIELD: 4 servings

GRILLED SEA BASS TACOS

The striped bass is a delicate, delicious choice for fish tacos. A great tip is to cook this fillet with the skin on—it helps keep the fish intact while grilling.

1. Season sea bass fillet with salt, pepper, ají amarillo powder, lime zest, and olive oil. Let sit for 10 minutes to allow flavors to meld.
2. Heat a grill over medium-high heat. Place sea bass on grill, and let cook for 2 minutes on each side.
3. Remove fish from grill and season with a squeeze of lime. Pull fillet apart for taco assembly.

TO BUILD:

Place the shredded red cabbage on top of a Soft Corn Tortilla, followed by the Grilled Sea Bass, Spicy Peach, Corn, and Tomato Pico, and Chipotle Crema. Serve with Seasoned Limes.

INGREDIENTS:

1 cup red cabbage, shredded

8 Soft Corn Tortillas (see recipe pg. 23)

Grilled Sea Bass (recipe below)

Spicy Peach, Corn, and Tomato Pico (see recipe pg. 85)

Chipotle Crema (see recipe pg. 104)

Seasoned Limes (see recipe pg. 332)

FOR THE GRILLED SEA BASS:

1½ pounds sea bass fillet, skinless

kosher salt

black pepper

½ teaspoon ají amarillo powder

zest of 1 whole lime

olive oil

CRACKLING CALAMARI WITH FIERY SALSA

These crispy calamari take on a spicy personality when dipped into the chile-hot salsa.

INGREDIENTS:

Fiery Tomato Salsa (recipe below)

Calamari (recipe on the right)

chopped parsley, to sprinkle

Seasoned Lemons (see recipe pg. 332)

FIERY TOMATO SALSA:

4 large ripe tomatoes, chopped

1 small red onion, coarsely chopped

5 cloves garlic, coarsely chopped

1 Serrano chile

2 tablespoons olive oil

1 jalapeño, sliced

1 tablespoon chipotle hot sauce

1 tablespoon oregano

¼ cup chopped fresh cilantro leaves

juice of 1 lime

kosher salt

pepper

FOR THE CALAMARI:

½ tablespoon ají amarillo paste

1 cup buttermilk

1 pound squid, cut into ½-inch rings

vegetable oil, for frying

2 cups precooked cornmeal

1 tablespoon ancho chile powder

½ tablespoon kosher salt, plus for finishing

2 eggs

MAKE THE FIERY TOMATO SALSA:

1. Quickly toss tomatoes, red onions, garlic, and chiles lightly in olive oil. Grill the tomatoes, onions, garlic, and chiles to achieve a smokier flavor.

2. In a molcajete (mortar and pestle), smash together the grilled ingredients. (Or quickly puree the mixture with a handheld immersion blender until it is rather smooth, but mostly chunky.) Simmer on the stovetop for an additional 10 to 15 minutes.

3. Add the hot sauce, oregano, cilantro, and lime juice. Season with salt and pepper, to taste.

MAKE THE CALAMARI:

1. In a medium bowl, combine ají amarillo paste and buttermilk. Add calamari rings and place calamari bowl in the refrigerator for 2 hours to marinate.

(recipe continues)

2. Heat a large, deep skillet, or fryer filled ⅓ of the way with vegetable oil to 350F degrees.

3. In a medium-size bowl, combine cornmeal, ancho chile powder, and salt. In a small bowl, beat eggs.

4. One by one, remove calamari from buttermilk and shake off excess. Dip calamari in egg, then toss in cornmeal mixture, press firmly to make sure cornmeal sticks to calamari.

5. Arrange calamari on a tray and put them in the freezer for 30 minutes to firm up the breading.

6. When ready to fry, take the calamari out of the freezer and, without letting them thaw, fry them for 1 minute or for as long as it takes for the calamari to float to the top. Remove from oil and place on paper towels to drain. Season with salt.

TO SERVE:

Arrange the calamari, Fiery Tomato Salsa, and Seasoned Lemons on a beautiful platter and enjoy.

PREP TIME: 30 minutes

TOTAL TIME: 1 hour

YIELD: 4 servings

SALTED COD

Salted codfish requires some prep work, as it needs to be soaked and rinsed, but it yields a comfort dish that's flavorful and satisfying. In this combo, the hot, salty cod contrasts with cool and crisp lettuce, creamy avocado and spicy crema.

1. Soak the salted cod overnight. The following day, change water every 30 minutes up to 7 times.
2. In a medium-size pot, boil the salted cod, allspice, and bay leaves in enough water to cover ingredients. Cook for 45 minutes at medium-low heat until tender.
3. Rinse the cod in cold water. Remove skin and bones.
4. In a sauté pan, heat olive oil on medium heat for about 2 minutes.
5. Add garlic and sauté for 30 seconds. Add onions and sauté for 1 minute. Add peppers and sauté for 2 minutes.
6. Add white wine and rinsed fish to pan. Cook over medium-low heat until wine is reduced, about 15 minutes.
7. Season with salt and pepper to taste. Sprinkle with parsley. Set aside.

TO SERVE:

Warm the Carrot Reinitas on a hot grill for a few seconds, or in the microwave with a damp towel for a few seconds. Serve the Salted Cod with avocado slices on top. On the side, serve the warm reinitas, Ají Amarillo Crema, and shredded lettuce.

INGREDIENTS:

8 warm Carrot Reinitas (see recipe pg. 20), to serve on the side

Salted Cod (recipe below)

fresh avocado, sliced

Ají Amarillo Crema (see recipe pg. 107), to serve on the side

shredded lettuce, to serve on the side

FOR THE SALTED COD:

1 pound salted cod

6 whole allspice berries

2 bay leaves

½ cup olive oil

8 cloves garlic, minced

1 large onion, julienned

1 cup red sweet bell peppers, julienned

½ cup white wine

kosher salt

pepper

½ cup parsley, finely chopped

GRILLED FISH TACOS

INGREDIENTS:

8 Blue Corn Tortillas (see recipe pg. 26)

Green Cabbage Slaw (see recipe pg. 125)

Grilled Grouper (see recipe below)

Pico de Gallo (see recipe pg. 67)

fresh avocado, sliced

fresh lime, wedges

FOR THE GRILLED GROUPER:

1 pound fresh grouper

kosher salt

freshly ground black pepper

This dish is probably one of the simplest in the book. It's also one of my favorites. These tacos are both light and decadent. When paired with cabbage slaw, avocado, and pico, this meaty, well-seasoned grouper makes a delicious filling for blue corn tortillas.

1. Prepare a hot charcoal or gas grill. Season grouper liberally with salt and pepper on both sides.
2. Place grouper on grill. Let cook for 4 minutes and turn on other side; let cook for another 4 minutes.
3. Remove fish from grill. With two forks, break apart grouper into bite-size pieces.

TO BUILD:

Warm the tortillas on the hot grill for a few seconds or in the microwave with a damp towel for a few seconds. Top each warm tortilla with Cabbage Slaw, grilled grouper, Pico de Gallo, and fresh avocado slices. Serve with a fresh lime wedge.

PREP TIME: 25 minutes

TOTAL TIME: 35 minutes

YIELD: 4 servings

PAN-SEARED MAHI MAHI

I love mahi mahi because it's a meaty fish with plenty of body to it. It stays intact when grilled or pan-seared, as in this recipe. And when you bite into it, it's almost like you're eating a steak.

1. In a medium-size bowl, combine lemon juice, olive oil, garlic, red pepper flakes, cilantro, and salt. Add mahi mahi fillets and marinate in the refrigerator for 20 minutes.

2. In a medium-size skillet, heat vegetable oil over medium-high heat. Once the pan is very hot, place fish in pan, reserving the marinade, and let cook for 2 minutes on one side.

3. Flip fish over and add white wine, reserved marinade, fish stock, and capers. Continue to cook another 2 minutes.

4. Add butter and let liquids reduce for another 4–6 minutes. Remove from heat and set aside.

TO BUILD:

Place the mahi mahi on top of the corn tortillas, followed by the Spicy Cucumber Tomato Pico de Gallo. Serve with a side of Grilled Green Tomatillo Sauce.

INGREDIENTS:

Pan-Seared Mahi Mahi (see recipe below)

8 Soft Corn Tortillas (see recipe pg. 23)

Spicy Cucumber Tomato Pico de Gallo (see recipe pg. 86)

Grilled Green Tomatillo Sauce (see recipe pg. 57)

FOR THE PAN-SEARED MAHI MAHI:

1 tablespoon lemon juice

3 tablespoons olive oil

¼ teaspoon garlic, minced

½ tablespoon red pepper flakes

2 tablespoons fresh cilantro, finely chopped

1 teaspoon kosher salt

1 pound mahi mahi, fillet, skinless

1 tablespoon vegetable oil

3 tablespoons white wine

3 tablespoons fish stock

1 tablespoon capers

½ tablespoon unsalted butter

ORANGE-DILL GRILLED SALMON

INGREDIENTS:

Orange-Dill Grilled Salmon (see recipe below)

Radish-Onion Slaw (see recipe below)

Chile-Lime Crema (see recipe pg. 110)

Carrot Reinitas, served in a basket (see recipe pg. 20)

FOR THE ORANGE-DILL GRILLED SALMON:

1 pound fresh salmon, skin on

kosher salt

fresh ground black pepper

FOR THE COMPOUND BUTTER:

3 tablespoons unsalted butter

1 teaspoon garlic, minced

1 teaspoon orange zest

1 tablespoon fresh dill, minced

FOR THE RADISH-ONION SLAW:

¼ cup radishes, cut into small matchsticks

¼ cup red onions, thinly sliced

1 teaspoon fresh dill, minced

3 teaspoons extra-virgin olive oil

½ teaspoon red chile peppers, diced small

½ teaspoon coconut vinegar

pinch of kosher salt

pinch of fresh ground black pepper

This zesty salmon, pulled apart into bite-size chunks, makes a flavorful topping for Carrot Reinitas. Paired with a Radish-Onion Slaw and some cooling Chile-Lime Crema, this combo serves as an ideal appetizer or party dish.

MAKE THE COMPOUND BUTTER:

In a small saucepan, melt butter with garlic over medium-low heat. Once butter is completely melted, remove from heat. Add orange zest and dill.

MAKE THE FISH:

1. Prepare a hot charcoal or gas grill. Season salmon liberally with salt and pepper on both sides.
2. Place salmon, flesh side down, on grill. Let cook for 4 minutes and turn on other side. With a small spoon, place some of the butter over the salmon and let cook for another 5 minutes.
3. Remove salmon from grill and pour remaining dill butter over the top.

MAKE THE RADISH-ONION SLAW:

In a small bowl, combine radishes, red onions, dill, extra-virgin olive oil, red chile peppers, coconut vinegar, salt, and pepper.

TO SERVE:

With two forks, break apart salmon into bite-size pieces. Place Radish-Onion Slaw on top of salmon. Serve with Chile-Lime Crema and a basket of Carrot Reinitas, and build your own salmon reinita.

PREP TIME: 25 minutes
TOTAL TIME: 30 minutes
YIELD: 6–8 servings

CRAB SALAD

What's better than creamy crab salad? Creamy crab salad that's cradled in an arepa. This salad pops with the flavors of red and green onions, red pepper, cilantro, mint, and jalapeño.

1. In a small bowl, combine mayonnaise, Dijon mustard, and lime juice.
2. In a large bowl, combine crabmeat, red onions, green onions, red peppers, cilantro, mint, and jalapeño.
3. Add mayonnaise-Dijon mix to crabmeat bowl and toss well to combine.

TO BUILD:

Stuff the arepa with the baby arugula, followed by the Crab Salad. Finish the layering with Crispy Onions.

INGREDIENTS:

6–8 Arepas (see recipe pg. 7)

1 cup baby arugula

Crab Salad (see recipe below)

Crispy Onions (see recipe pg. 338)

FOR THE CRAB SALAD:

½ cup mayonnaise

1 tablespoon Dijon mustard

2 tablespoons lime juice

1 pound jumbo lump crabmeat

½ cup red onions, diced small

¼ cup green onions, diced small

¼ cup red peppers, diced small

2 tablespoons fresh cilantro, finely chopped

1 tablespoon fresh mint, finely chopped

1 tablespoon jalapeño, minced

1 teaspoon kosher salt

PREP TIME: 30 minutes
TOTAL TIME: 35 minutes
YIELD: 4 servings

SPICY MANGO–GLAZED KING CRAB

INGREDIENTS:

4 Sweet Corn Cakes (see recipe pg. 294)

Cherry Pepper Pico de Gallo (see recipe pg. 70)

Spicy Mango–Glazed King Crab (recipe follows)

FOR THE SPICY MANGO GLAZE:

½ cup mango juice

1 tablespoon Sriracha sauce

2 tablespoons unsalted butter

FOR THE SPICY MANGO–GLAZED KING CRAB:

vegetable oil (enough to fill ⅓ of pan), for frying

2 eggs

1 cup club soda

2 cups all-purpose flour

1 tablespoon kosher salt

½ tablespoon cayenne pepper

2 tablespoons black sesame seeds

2 king crab legs, out of shell and cut into 3-inch pieces

¼ cup Spicy Mango Glaze

Crispy, glazed crab chunks find a sweet home in cachapa corn cakes. A layer of Cherry Pepper Pico de Gallo brings all the flavors together.

MAKE THE SPICY MANGO GLAZE:

In a small saucepan over medium heat, combine mango juice, Sriracha, and butter. Set aside.

MAKE THE SPICY MANGO–GLAZED KING CRAB:

1. In a large, deep skillet or fryer, heat vegetable oil to 350F degrees.
2. In a medium-size bowl, whisk eggs and then add club soda.
3. In another medium bowl, mix together flour, salt, cayenne pepper, and sesame seeds.
4. One by one, dip crab pieces in egg mixture, toss in seasoned flour, and shake off excess flour.
5. Carefully drop crab in oil and cook for 2 to 3 minutes, until golden brown.
6. Remove from oil, place on paper towels to absorb oil, and season with salt.
7. Pour mango glaze in a bowl, turning slowly to cover the inside of the bowl. Gently toss king crab in bowl to evenly coat with glaze.

COMPOSE THE DISH:

Place the Cherry Pepper Pico de Gallo on the corn cakes, then top with the Spicy Mango–Glazed King Crab.

PREP TIME: 30 minutes

TOTAL TIME: 35 minutes

YIELD: 6 servings

PAN-SEARED CHIPOTLE SCALLOPS

Lemon zest is my secret weapon when I want to give scallops a great aroma without overcooking them the way lemon juice can. The trick to the perfect sear on the scallop is high temperature.

1. In a medium-size skillet, heat vegetable oil on high heat.
2. Season scallops with salt and pepper and place in skillet with the lemon zest. Let them cook for 1 minute on one side, then flip them and cook another 30 seconds to 1 minute. Remove scallops from pan and set aside.

TO BUILD:

Top each Carrot Telita with the Citrus Carrot Slaw, then the Chipotle Crema. Finish by topping them with the Pan-Seared Chipotle Scallops.

INGREDIENTS:

6 Crispy Carrot Telitas (flat breads; see recipe pg. 13)

Citrus Carrot Slaw (see recipe pg. 131)

Chipotle Crema (see recipe pg. 104)

Pan-Seared Chipotle Scallops (recipe below)

FOR THE PAN-SEARED CHIPOTLE SCALLOPS:

1 tablespoon vegetable oil

6 large scallops, cleaned

kosher salt

black pepper

zest of 1 lemon

PREP TIME: 10 minutes
TOTAL TIME: 30 minutes
YIELD: 8 servings

CHILE-CRUSTED JUMBO SHRIMP

The layers of flavors in these spicy shrimp tostadas build upon one another, from the seasoned panko crumbs to the ancho- and coriander-laced egg dip. The reward is a complex, heady bite.

INGREDIENTS:

Garbanzo Bean Spread (see recipe pg. 41)

8 Tostadas (see recipe pg. 25)

Chile-Crusted Jumbo Shrimp (recipe below)

FOR THE CHILE-CRUSTED JUMBO SHRIMP:

2 whole eggs

1 teaspoon ancho chile powder

1 teaspoon ground coriander

½ tablespoon kosher salt

2 cups panko bread crumbs

1 teaspoon paprika

8 jumbo shrimp, tail on, cleaned and deveined

1. In a medium-size bowl, whisk together eggs, ancho chile powder, coriander, and salt.
2. In another bowl, combine panko bread crumbs and paprika.
3. Dip each jumbo shrimp into egg mixture and shake off excess.
4. Coat shrimp in panko crumbs, pressing lightly to ensure crumbs stick to each shrimp. Repeat egg and panko steps once more.
5. Place panko-crusted jumbo shrimp on a plate or baking sheet and refrigerate for 30 minutes.
6. Remove from refrigerator and let sit for 20 minutes before frying.
7. Carefully drop shrimp into fryer. Cook for 3 minutes. Remove shrimp from oil with a slotted spoon, place on a rack to drain, and season with salt.

TO BUILD:

Put the Garbanzo Bean Spread on the Tostada and top with Chile-Crusted Jumbo Shrimp.

PREP TIME: 30 minutes
TOTAL TIME: 35 minutes
YIELD: 6 servings

GRILLED SHRIMP TELITA

INGREDIENTS:

6 fried Beet Telitas (see recipe pg. 11)

Black Bean Spread (see recipe pg. 39)

Spicy Green Papaya Slaw (see recipe pg. 128)

Grilled Shrimp (recipe below)

FOR THE GRILLED SHRIMP:

18 large shrimp, cleaned and deveined

1 tablespoon olive oil

1 teaspoon ground chile de arbol

1 teaspoon ground coriander

1 teaspoon kosher salt

1 whole lemon

These simply grilled shrimp, spiced with coriander and chile de arbol, are nestled into crispy Beet Telitas atop a bed of Black Bean Spread. A heavenly Green Papaya Slaw adds crunch and spicy notes to the bite.

1. Skewer shrimp, placing three shrimp per skewer. Brush olive oil on both sides of shrimp.
2. Season both sides with chile de arbol, coriander, and salt.
3. Prepare a hot charcoal or gas grill. Place skewers on grill and cook for 3 minutes on each side, turning once.
4. Remove shrimp skewers from grill and squeeze fresh lemon juice on each of the shrimp.

TO BUILD:

Put Black Bean Spread on each Beet Telita, then top spread with Spicy Green Papaya Slaw. Complete the layers by adding three grilled shrimp to each telita.

PREP TIME: 30 minutes
TOTAL TIME: 35 minutes
YIELD: 6 servings

ANGRY SHRIMP

This is one saucy tamal dish: red-pepper-infused and topped with a spicy sauté of shrimp, aromatics and spices.

1. In a large skillet, heat oil over medium-high heat. Sauté the onions, garlic, and chile cachucha (or ají dulce) until onions are translucent.
2. Add jalapeño, tomatoes, chile de arbol, ground coriander, ground ginger, tomato paste, and white wine.
3. Add shrimp, sugar, capers, and salt. Sauté for 3–5 minutes.
4. Remove from heat and mix in parsley and cilantro.

TO BUILD:

Place 1 Roasted Red Pepper Tamal on the center of a plate. Unfasten the corn husks and carefully (it's hot) open the tamal. Spoon the Angry Shrimp and its sauce over the center of the tamal. Sprinkle with fresh parsley.

INGREDIENTS:

6 Roasted Red Pepper Tamales (see recipe pg. 34)

Angry Shrimp (recipe below)

¼ cup fresh parsley, chopped

FOR THE ANGRY SHRIMP:

2 tablespoons vegetable oil

½ cup onions, diced small

2 tablespoons garlic, minced

½ cup cachucha or ají dulce chile, diced small

¼ cup red jalapeños, minced

½ cup fresh tomatoes, diced small

½ tablespoon ground chile de arbol

1 teaspoon ground coriander

½ tablespoon ground ginger

1½ tablespoons tomato paste

1 cup white wine

1 pound large shrimp, cleaned and deveined

1 tablespoon sugar

2 tablespoons capers

1½ teaspoons kosher salt

1½ tablespoons fresh parsley, finely chopped

1 tablespoon fresh cilantro, finely chopped

PREP TIME: 10 minutes
TOTAL TIME: 15 minutes
YIELD: 4-6 servings

INGREDIENTS:

Shrimp and Tomato Cocktail (recipe below)

Plantain Chips (recipe below)

FOR THE SHRIMP AND TOMATO COCKTAIL:

1 pound cooked and chilled medium shrimp, peeled, deveined, tails removed, chopped into bite-size pieces

½ cup shallots, diced small

½ cup celery, diced small

1 cup cucumber, seeded and diced small

1 jalapeño, minced

1 cup tomato, seeded, diced small, with juice

½ cup fresh cilantro, finely chopped

juice of 1 lime

1½ cups tomato juice

½ cup ketchup

1 tablespoon hot sauce

2 teaspoons kosher salt

1 teaspoon pepper

1 avocado, cut into cubes

FOR THE PLANTAIN CHIPS:

2 whole large green plantains, peeled

vegetable oil for frying (to fill ⅓ of skillet)

kosher salt

NEW CLASSIC SHRIMP COCKTAIL

Here's an appetizer that revs the palate. Hot sauce and jalapeño give this shrimp cocktail a spicy kick, while the tomatoes lend sweetness. A side serving of hot, crispy plantain chips completes the bite.

1. In a large bowl, place shrimp, shallots, celery, cucumber, jalapeño, tomatoes, cilantro, lime juice, tomato juice, ketchup, and hot sauce. Toss well to combine all ingredients.
2. To serve, season with salt, pepper, and hot sauce. Gently fold in avocado cubes.

TO MAKE THE PLANTAIN CHIPS:

1. Slice plantains diagonally, using mandolin or vegetable slicer, $\frac{1}{16}$ of an inch thick.
2. In a large skillet, heat oil over high heat to reach 350F degrees.
3. Add plantain slices to oil and fry for 5 minutes until crispy and golden brown.
4. Remove plantain chips with slotted spoon and allow them to drain on paper towels. Season immediately with kosher salt and serve hot.

TO BUILD:

Serve the Shrimp and Tomato Cocktail with a side of Plantain chips.

SWEET POTATO AREPAS WITH SMOKED SALMON

This is my take on a brunch taco. These sweet arepas are the worthy vessel for the salty and smoky notes of salmon and caviar, the richness of poached eggs and crème fraîche and the sparkle of lemon. A world of flavor in one bite.

MAKE THE DILL CREAM:

In a small bowl, stir the crème fraîche (or sour cream) together with the dill and lemon juice. Season with salt and black pepper, and sprinkle with the chives. Refrigerate until ready to serve.

MAKE THE SWEET POTATO AREPA:

1. In a medium bowl, mix the sweet potato, chives, flour, baking powder, vegetable oil, salt, and black pepper.
2. Divide the dough in equal parts and make patties, about 4 ounces each.
3. In a large nonstick skillet, place enough vegetable oil to cover the bottom of the pan, and heat to medium-high.
4. Place the arepas in the hot oil and fry until they are golden on the bottom, about 4 minutes. Flip the arepas and cook until golden, about 4 minutes longer. Repeat with the remaining arepas.

TO BUILD:

Arrange the arepas on a platter. Top them with baby arugula, then with a few slices of salmon, one egg, a dollop of Dill Cream, and caviar.

PREP TIME: 20 minutes

TOTAL TIME: 30 minutes

YIELD: 4 servings

INGREDIENTS:

1 cup baby arugula

½ pound thinly sliced smoked salmon

4 poached eggs

Dill Cream (see recipe below)

2 ounces black caviar

FOR THE DILL CREAM:

½ cup crème fraîche or sour cream

1 teaspoon dill, chopped

1 teaspoon fresh lemon juice

kosher salt

freshly ground black pepper

1 tablespoon chives, finely sliced

FOR THE SWEET POTATO AREPA:

2 medium sweet potatoes, peeled, cooked and mashed

1 tablespoon chives, finely sliced

½ cup masa arepa flour

1 tablespoon baking powder

1 tablespoon vegetable oil

2 teaspoons kosher salt

¼ teaspoon freshly ground black pepper

vegetable oil for frying

PREP TIME: 10 minutes

TOTAL TIME: 25 minutes

YIELD: 8 servings

INGREDIENTS:

1 medium jícama

Grilled Maine Lobster
(recipe follows)

Ají Amarillo Crema (see
recipe pg. 107)

Spicy Pickled Onions (see
recipe pg. 98)

FOR THE COMPOUND BUTTER:

1 cup unsalted butter

½ tablespoon garlic, minced

zest of 1 whole lemon

1 teaspoon red pepper
flakes

2 teaspoons fresh parsley
leaves, minced

FOR THE GRILLED MAINE LOBSTER:

four 6-ounce lobster tails

½ cup Compound Butter
(recipe follows)

4 wood or metal skewers

GRILLED LOBSTER TACO

*This taco is a study of contrasts: buttery lobster meets Spicy
Pickled Onions, and a tangy Ají Amarillo Crema atop a cool,
crunchy jícama shell. Using jícama as a tortilla shell gives this
taco tons of texture.*

1. In a small saucepan, melt butter with garlic over medium-
   low heat. Once butter is completely melted, remove from
   heat. Add lemon zest, red pepper flakes, and parsley and
   set aside.
2. Preheat grill to medium-high heat. Using kitchen shears,
   cut through the shell of the lobster tail straight down the
   middle, lengthwise, exposing the flesh. Insert a skewer
   through the underside of the lobster tail so it does not curl
   on the grill.
3. Place each lobster tail on a sheet of aluminum foil (large
   enough to wrap the tail). With a small spoon, pour butter
   into the incision made on the top of the lobster shell. Coat
   the top, bottom, and ends of lobster tail with butter and
   wrap in foil.
4. Grill 15 minutes or until lobster meat is opaque. Remove
   from heat and let stand for 5 minutes. Slice lobster into
   ½-inch slices and pour remaining butter over top.

PREP THE JÍCAMA:

Take one whole medium-size jícama and scrub it well to
wash off residue. Using a mandolin on the ⅛-inch setting,
slice the jícama.

BUILD THE TACO:

On a plate, place one slice of jícama and top with Grilled
Maine Lobster and a dollop of Ají Amarillo Cream. Crown
with Spicy Pickled Onions.

LOBSTER GUACAMOLE

If you enjoy a chunky-style guacamole, you'll love this rendition, thanks to one stellar ingredient: Maine lobster! This guac can be served with any reinita recipe in this book, or simply with a side of tortilla chips.

1. In a molcajete (mortar and pestle), combine garlic, 1 teaspoon onions, cilantro and salt. Muddle to combine well.
2. Add avocados, the remaining ½ cup of onions, tomatoes, jalapeño, lime juice, lemon juice, and extra-virgin olive oil. Smash all ingredients to achieve a chunky guacamole consistency.
3. Fold in lobster pieces and cilantro. Serve in molcajete or in serving bowl with a side of Cilantro Reinitas.

INGREDIENTS:

1 teaspoon garlic, minced

½ cup plus 1 teaspoon onions, diced small

4 tablespoons fresh cilantro, finely chopped

½ teaspoon kosher salt

2 whole avocados, peeled and cubed

½ cup tomatoes, diced small

1 tablespoon jalapeño, diced small

1 tablespoon lime juice

½ tablespoon lemon juice

1 tablespoon extra-virgin olive oil

six 8-ounce grilled Maine lobster tails, cut into ½-inch cubes (See Grilled Lobster Taco recipe on pg. 236)

8 Cilantro Reinitas (see recipe pg. 19)

CHAPTER 11

MEATS

Prepare for a festival of meats—that's how I see the collection of celebration-worthy beef and lamb dishes featured in this chapter.

We'll go from barbecue brisket to Brazilian steak in a hot minute and showcase the ways we can bring hearty flavors to just about any cut of meat. The resilience of beef invites great, smoky rubs, glazes, and chars. It also encourages a variety of cooking techniques, from low-and-slow braises to quick-fire searing methods.

The results? Delicious, robust fillings and toppings for tacos, arepas, tostadas, tamales, and any other kind of masa vessel you crave.

RECIPES

PREP TIME: 10 minutes

TOTAL TIME: 20 minutes

YIELD: 4 servings

THE CLASSIC HARD-SHELL TACO

The secret set of ingredients in this ground beef recipe is in the taco spice blend I use to season the meat. The end result is a taco filling with unexpected notes of coriander and piquín chile.

INGREDIENTS:

1 Ground Beef (see recipe below)

8 Hard-Shell Tortillas (see recipe on pg. 23, or store-bought is fine)

1½ cup shredded iceberg lettuce

1 cup of cheddar cheese, shredded

1 Pico de Gallo (see recipe pg. 67)

Chile de Arbol Sauce (optional, see pg. 53)

TACO SPICE BLEND:

½ teaspoon garlic powder

½ teaspoon onion powder

1½ tablespoons chili powder

2 teaspoons cornstarch

1 tablespoon ground cumin

2 teaspoons kosher salt

1 teaspoon paprika

1 teaspoon ground coriander

½ teaspoon chile piquín powder

FOR THE GROUND BEEF:

¼ cup vegetable oil

1 cup onion, chopped

4 whole garlic cloves, minced

¼ cup chile cachucha (sweet chile), chopped

1 pound ground beef

Taco Spice Blend (see above recipe above)

¾ cup beef stock

1. In a small bowl, make the Taco Spice Blend by whisking together garlic powder, onion powder, chili powder, cornstarch, ground cumin, salt, paprika, coriander, and chile piquín powder.
2. In a medium-size skillet, heat vegetable oil over medium-high heat.
3. Add onions to skillet and cook for 3 minutes, until translucent. Add garlic and cook for an additional minute. Add sweet chiles and cook for 1 minute.
4. Add ground beef to skillet, stirring constantly to break apart beef and brown evenly. Cook beef for 5 minutes, then add Taco Spice Blend and stir well to combine.
5. Once Taco Spice Blend is thoroughly mixed with the beef, add the beef stock to the skillet. Cook until liquid reduces, about 4 minutes.
6. Preheat the oven to 375F degrees. Heat taco shells for about 5 minutes.

BUILD THE TACOS:

Spoon about ¼ cup of the ground beef mixture into each shell. Top with shredded lettuce, cheese, and Pico de Gallo. If desired, serve with a side of Chile de Arbol Sauce.

PILONCILLO TELITAS WITH ASADO NEGRO

PREP TIME: 15 minutes

TOTAL TIME: 2 hours and 15 minutes

YIELD: 4 servings

The pure, unrefined sugar in the piloncillo and rich malta beverage give the beef in this dish a deep sweetness that's tempered by garlic, zesty mustard, and beef broth in a two-hour braise. The flavors of the braised meat are enhanced by the anise notes in its vessel: an Anise-and-Piloncillo Telita.

INGREDIENTS:

8 crispy Anise-and-Piloncillo Telitas (see recipe pg. 10)

1 Asado Negro (see recipe below)

1 Green Guasacaca sauce (see recipe pg 94)

1 cup queso fresco, grated

¼ cup red onions, thinly sliced

MARINADE:

¼ cup onion, diced

¼ cup chile cachucha (sweet chile), diced

2 teaspoons kosher salt

6 whole garlic cloves, minced

¾ cup red vermouth

¾ cup malta beverage

3 tablespoons Worcestershire sauce

1 tablespoon Dijon mustard

1 teaspoon ground cumin

1 teaspoon dried oregano

FOR THE ASADO NEGRO:

2 pounds chuck or bottom round beef

FOR BRAISING:

¼ cup vegetable oil

¼ cup onions, diced

¼ cup red peppers, diced

¼ cup chile cachucha (sweet chile), diced

¼ cup leeks, green parts only, diced

3 tablespoons piloncillo or panela (pure, unrefined sugar), grated

1 cup beef broth

2 whole bay leaves

1 teaspoon salt

1 teaspoon fresh ground black pepper

1. In a large bowl, combine marinade ingredients.
2. With a sharp knife, make incisions in the meat and add meat to marinade. Cover meat with marinade and refrigerate for at least 2½ hours or overnight.
3. In a large oven-safe, deep skillet or pot, heat vegetable oil on medium-high heat.
4. Remove the meat from the marinade, reserving liquid for later use. Place meat in hot skillet and sear on each side, about 5 minutes.
5. Remove the meat from the skillet and set it aside. To the skillet, add onions, red peppers, chile cachucha, leeks,

(recipe continues)

and piloncillo. Sauté until piloncillo begins to caramelize, about 1 minute.

6. Return meat to the skillet and continue cooking for 5 minutes. Once meat has caramelized, add the remaining marinade, beef broth, and bay leaves. Season with salt and pepper.

7. Bring ingredients to a boil, cover, reduce heat, and let simmer for 2 hours or place in a 325F degree oven for 2 hours.

8. Once the meat has cooked through, remove it from the pan, leaving the sauce. Blend the sauce in a blender or with an immersion blender.

9. Return the sauce to the skillet and bring it to a boil over medium-high heat.

10. Slice beef against the grain into thin, even slices.

11. Place slices into the simmering sauce, lowering the heat to medium and allowing the sauce to reduce by half, about 15–20 minutes.

TO BUILD:

Top a Telita with the Asado Negro meat. Spoon the Green Guasacaca sauce over it and sprinkle with queso fresco. Garnish the dish with a few slices of freshly cut red onion.

PREP TIME: 20 minutes

TOTAL TIME: 1 hour

YIELD: 6 servings

PULLED BEEF NACHOS

This dish is not only shareable—it's adaptable. You can use as much or as little of the Pulled Beef and the Black Beans with Queso Fundido as you want. Set aside whatever you're not using and freeze it for later.

INGREDIENTS:

1 bag of corn tortilla chips

1 bag of blue corn tortilla chips

1 pound Pulled Beef (recipe follows)

1 Black Beans with Queso Fundido (see recipe pg. 307)

2 cups Cherry Pepper Pico de Gallo (see recipe pg. 70)

FOR THE PULLED BEEF:

2 pounds flank steak

8 cups water

3 cloves garlic

½ medium onion

1 small carrot, diced small

1 celery stick, diced small

2 bay leaves

SOFRITO INGREDIENTS:

2 tablespoons extra-virgin olive oil

⅓ cup onion, chopped

4 whole garlic cloves, minced

¼ cup ají dulce, diced

¼ cup red bell pepper, diced

⅓ cup leeks, diced

¼ green onions, diced

½ tablespoon ground cumin

1 teaspoon dried oregano

2 tablespoons tomato paste

1 tablespoon Worcestershire sauce

1 tablespoon capers

TO SIMMER AND SEASON:

2½ cups beef stock

2 teaspoons kosher salt

1 teaspoon fresh ground black pepper

1. In a medium-size stockpot, place flank steak with water, garlic, onion, carrot, celery, and bay leaves. Bring to a boil and cover. Reduce heat and cook until meat is tender, about 1 hour.
2. Remove pot from heat. Strain the liquid and reserve 2½ cups of the beef stock. Allow meat to cool. Shred meat with hands or forks.
3. In a large skillet, heat olive oil over medium high heat. Sauté onions for 1 minute, add garlic, and cook for 1 minute. Add ají dulce, red bell peppers, leeks, and green onions. Cook for 3 to 4 minutes until vegetables are translucent.
4. Stir to combine ground cumin, dried oregano, tomato paste, Worcestershire sauce, and capers. Add shredded beef and beef stock. Season with salt and pepper.
5. Cook uncovered on medium heat, stirring occasionally for about 10 minutes, until most of the liquid has reduced.
6. Preheat the oven to 350F degrees. On a large oven-safe platter, arrange the tortilla chips.
7. Spoon the Pulled Beef mixture evenly over the chips. Pour the Black Beans with Queso Fundido on top.
8. Place the oven-safe platter in the oven for 5 minutes, until the cheese melts and bubbles. Remove from the oven and sprinkle with the Cherry Pepper Pico de Gallo. Serve immediately.

PREP TIME: 10 minutes

TOTAL TIME: 20 minutes

YIELD: 4 servings

TRADITIONAL GROUND BEEF TOSTADA

INGREDIENTS:

8 corn tostadas (see recipe pg. 25)

1 Garbanzo Bean Spread (see recipe pg. 41)

1 Ground Beef (see recipe for Classic Hard-Shell Tacos pg. 242)

1½ cups Monterey Jack cheese, shredded

⅓ cup Lime Crema (see recipe pg. 106)

1½ cups shredded lettuce

¼ cup fresh cilantro leaves

1 bottle of hot sauce (optional)

I love a good tostada, especially one in which each layer brings its own flavor personality. In this recipe, those layers include a rich chickpea spread, a well-seasoned ground beef filling and a lime-infused crema.

1. On each tostada, put Garbanzo Bean Spread. Spoon the Ground Beef on top. Add a sprinkling of cheese and a drizzle of Lime Crema.
2. Top with lettuce, cilantro and hot sauce, if desired. Serve immediately.

BBQ BEEF BRISKET AREPA

PREP TIME: 20 minutes

TOTAL TIME: 5 hours;
45 minutes to 1 hour in
pressure cooker

YIELD: 4 servings

I cook this beef brisket low and slow in a homemade barbecue sauce that's sweet, smoky, and acidic. After a few hours in a slow cooker, it becomes a sublime filling for a fresh arepa. Add crunchy slaw for cool, crisp contrast.

INGREDIENTS:

4 Arepas (see recipe pg. 7)

BBQ Beef Brisket (see recipe below)

Green Cabbage Slaw (see recipe pg. 125)

FOR THE BBQ BEEF BRISKET:

1 tablespoon garlic powder

1 tablespoon onion powder

1 tablespoon ground cumin

1 teaspoon ancho chile powder

2 tablespoons smoked paprika

3 tablespoons dark brown sugar

1 tablespoon salt

1 teaspoon black pepper

2½ pounds beef brisket

FOR THE BARBECUE SAUCE:

1 tablespoon olive oil

¼ cup yellow onion, finely chopped

4 garlic cloves, minced

1 cup ketchup

¼ cup packed dark brown sugar

1 cup water

¼ cup apple cider vinegar

3 tablespoons Worcestershire sauce

2 chipotles in adobo sauce, finely chopped

1 teaspoon freshly ground black pepper

SHORTCUT: Use a pressure cooker to cut cooking time by half.

1. In a medium-size bowl, combine garlic powder, onion powder, cumin, ancho chile powder, smoked paprika, dark brown sugar, salt, and pepper.
2. Cut beef brisket into 2 equal-size pieces about ¼-inch thick, across the grain. Place brisket in the dry rub and coat all sides evenly.

MAKE THE BARBECUE SAUCE:

1. In a large, deep skillet with a lid or in a slow cooker, heat olive oil over medium-high heat. Add onion and garlic and sauté for 2 minutes.
2. Add remaining barbecue sauce ingredients. Stir ingredients together and simmer for 3–4 minutes.

(recipe continues)

COOK THE BRISKET:

1. Add brisket to barbecue sauce and cover the skillet tightly with a lid or with aluminum foil. Cook over low heat for 4–5 hours, turning the brisket over every 45 minutes to 1 hour. (If using a slow cooker, add the beef to the sauce and set the cooker on low for 8 hours or high for 4 hours. If using a pressure cooker, add beef to sauce and cook for 45 minutes to 1 hour.)

2. Remove the brisket and place on a clean cutting board. Let sauce cool slightly, then pour it into a blender. Blend until smooth.

3. Return sauce to skillet and bring to a boil. (If using an immersion blender, blend sauce in skillet and bring to a boil.) Let the sauce reduce by half, about 10 minutes.

4. With a sharp knife, slice the brisket against the grain into ¼-inch slices. Pour reduced sauce over slices and set aside.

TO BUILD:

Using a sharp knife, split open a still warm arepa like a pita pocket, making a slit in the top and wiggling a knife into the center of the arepa to create a pocket. Stuff the arepas with the BBQ Beef Brisket and top with Green Cabbage Slaw.

MORCILLA PUFFY TACOS

Hearty blood sausage is the star ingredient in these puffy tacos. A layer of Fava Bean Spread adds richness, while Pickled Watermelon Radishes add great crunch and acidity.

PREPARE BLOOD SAUSAGE:

1. In a medium-size frying pan, heat vegetable oil over medium-high heat. Sauté the blood sausage, onions, and jalapeño for 4 minutes.

2. Remove pan from heat. Add red onion and cilantro. Season with salt and pepper, and set aside.

BUILD THE TACO:

Put the Fava Bean Spread onto 4 Puffy Tortillas. Top with the prepared Morcilla. The finishing touches are cilantro and Pickled Watermelon Radishes.

PREP TIME: 10 minutes

TOTAL TIME: 15 minutes

YIELD: 4 servings

INGREDIENTS:

Fava Bean Spread (see recipe pg. 40)

4 Puffy Tortillas (see recipe pg. 29)

Blood Sausage (see recipe below)

Pickled Watermelon Radishes (see recipe pg. 98)

MORCILLA (BLOOD SAUSAGE):

¼ cup vegetable oil

2 blood sausages, sliced about 1-inch thick

½ cup yellow onion, diced

1 whole jalapeño, sliced into thin rounds

¼ cup red onions, diced

¼ cup fresh cilantro, finely chopped

1 teaspoon kosher salt

1 teaspoon fresh ground black pepper

½ tablespoon fresh cilantro, finely chopped, to garnish

PREP TIME: 10 minutes

TOTAL TIME: 25 minutes

YIELD: 4 servings

COFFEE-RUBBED STEAK TACO WITH BLACK BEAN SUCCOTASH

Here's a taco that proves coffee is not just for breakfast—it makes a fantastic rub for flavorful cuts of beef. In this recipe, I rub a spicy blend of coffee, spices, and chile de arbol on rib eye steaks for a gorgeously seared result.

INGREDIENTS:

Crispy Cilantro Telitas (see recipe pg. 12)

Coffee-Rubbed Rib Eye (see recipe below)

Black Bean Succotash (see recipe pg. 304)

sprigs of fresh cilantro

1 jalapeño, thinly sliced in wheels

FOR THE COFFEE RUB:

¼ cup ancho chile powder

¼ cup finely ground espresso

2 tablespoons paprika

2 tablespoons dark brown sugar

1 tablespoon dry mustard

1 tablespoon kosher salt

1 tablespoon ground black pepper

1 tablespoon ground coriander

1 tablespoon dried oregano

2 teaspoons ground ginger

2 teaspoons chile de arbol powder

2 tablespoons vegetable oil

salt and coarsely ground black pepper

FOR THE COFFEE-RUBBED RIB EYE MEAT:

2 rib eye steaks, bone-in or boneless, 2-inches thick, about 1½ pounds each

kosher salt, to season

freshly ground black pepper, to season

MAKE THE RUB:

In a bowl, whisk all coffee-rub ingredients together.

PREPARE THE STEAK:

1. Preheat oven to 425F degrees. Preheat a cast-iron pan with vegetable oil over high heat. Season 1 side of the steak liberally with salt and pepper. Turn steak over and press coffee rub into meat. Spread coffee rub evenly between steaks.

2. In a cast-iron skillet over medium-high heat, sear the steak, rub side down, until golden brown, about 2 minutes. Flip the steak over and cook for another 2 minutes.

3. Place skillet with steaks in the oven and roast to medium-rare doneness, about 5 minutes. Remove and let rest 5 minutes before slicing. Set aside.

BUILD THE TACOS:

Top the Crispy Cilantro Telitas with the sliced rib eye steak, then with the Black Bean Succotash. Add a sprig of cilantro and jalapeño slices.

CHAR-GRILLED STEAK TACOS

PREP TIME: 20 minutes
TOTAL TIME: 30 minutes
YIELD: 8 servings

These tacos are a cinch to make. Just make sure your grill is hot and your steaks are generously seasoned with salt and pepper.

GRILL THE STEAK:

1. Prepare a hot charcoal or gas grill.
2. Season churrasco liberally on both sides with salt and pepper. Place steak on hot grill and cook without moving until there are grill marks, 4–5 minutes.
3. Turn steak over and cook another 2–3 minutes for medium-rare, 4 minutes for medium, 5 minutes or longer for medium well.
4. Remove churrasco from grill and let it rest for 2–3 minutes before slicing.
5. Slice the steak against the grain into 4-inch-long and ¼-inch-thick slices. Set aside.

MAKE THE SMOTHERED ONIONS:

In a medium-size pan, add butter and onions and cook on medium-high heat for about 2 minutes until onions are translucent.

BUILD THE TACOS:

Top each Black Bean Telita with Grilled Churrasco slices. Place Smothered Onions on top of the steak. Crown with the Avocado Croutons. Serve with a Seasoned Lemon wedge on the side.

INGREDIENTS:

8 Black Bean Telitas (see recipe pg. 14)

Grilled Churrasco (see recipe below)

Smothered Onions (recipe follows)

Avocado Croutons (see recipe pg. 335)

Seasoned Lemon (see recipe pg. 332)

FOR THE CHAR-GRILLED CHURRASCO STEAK:

2 pounds churrasco (skirt) steak

kosher salt

fresh ground black pepper

FOR THE SMOTHERED ONIONS:

2 tablespoons butter

2 cups white onions, thinly sliced

PREP TIME: 20 minutes
TOTAL TIME: 30 minutes
YIELD: 4–6 servings

NEW YORK STRIP STEAK TACOS

INGREDIENTS:

8 to 12 warm flour tortillas

New York Strip Steak
(recipe below)

Padron chiles

Kale Slaw (see recipe
pg. 121)

Salsa Verde Cruda (see
recipe pg. 61)

Chile de Arbol Sauce
(optional, see recipe pg. 53)

FOR THE STEAK:

2 pounds New York Strip
Steak, 1-inch thick

kosher salt

fresh ground black pepper

FOR THE CHILES:

12 Padron chiles

½ cup olive oil

kosher salt

fresh ground black pepper

Pair this steak with a batch of nicely charred, well-seasoned Padron chiles for a sublime result. Padron chiles can be quite sneaky—it is said that one in ten of them is very spicy. If you're lucky, you'll find that one hot chile!

1. Prepare a hot charcoal or gas grill. Season the steak liberally on both sides with salt and pepper.
2. Place steak on hot grill and cook without moving until there are grill marks, 4–5 minutes. Turn New York Strip Steak over and cook another 2–3 minutes for medium rare, 4 minutes for medium, 5 minutes or longer for medium-well.
3. Remove steak from the grill and let it rest for at least 3 minutes. Once rested, slice the steak against the grain into ¼-inch-thick slices.

PREPARE THE CHILES:

Toss the Padron chiles with olive oil, salt, and pepper. Place seasoned chiles on the hot grill and cook for 1–2 minutes on each side, until charred all around. Remove from grill and set aside until ready to serve.

BUILD THE TACOS:

Warm the flour tortillas on the grill for 20 seconds. Top each tortilla with steak slices, then slaw, then 1 or 2 Padron chiles. Serve the tacos with Salsa Verde Cruda on the side.

PREP TIME: 10 minutes

TOTAL TIME: 20 minutes

YIELD: 6 servings

BRAZILIAN-STYLE TACOS

Ever been to a Brazilian rodizio restaurant, the kind where servers in gaucho outfits parade around with skewered slabs of grilled meats? If so, you might know that the picanha cut is a Brazilian favorite. While you may not find meat that's labeled picanha at your local market, you can ask your butcher for a top sirloin cap or a tritip steak, which works well in this recipe.

GRILL THE STEAK:

1. Prepare a hot charcoal or gas grill. Season picanha liberally on both sides with salt and pepper.
2. Place picanha on grill and cook without moving for about 4–5 minutes. Turn picanha over and cook another 2–3 minutes for medium rare, 4 minutes for medium, 5 minutes or longer for medium-well.

MAKE THE BANANA FAROFA:

1. In a medium-size skillet, heat oil over medium-low heat and add onions, garlic, and salt.
2. Add banana and manioc flour. Continue to stir to avoid burning the flour.
3. Add butter and continue to cook for about 4 minutes over low heat. The flour should toast to a light brown color. Remove from heat and garnish with cilantro.

BUILD THE TACOS:

Warm the flour tortillas on a hot grill for 20 seconds. Top the warmed flour tortillas with the picanha slices, the Banana Farofa, and the Brazilian Pico.

INGREDIENTS:

12 Crispy Black Bean Telitas (see recipe pg. 14)

Picanha, or top sirloin cap, steak (see recipe below)

Banana Farofa (see recipe below)

Brazilian Pico de Gallo (see recipe pg. 69)

Spicy Rocoto Sauce (optional on the side, see recipe pg. 63)

FOR THE PICANHA STEAK:

2 pounds picanha (top sirloin cap or tri-tip), cut into 2-inch steaks

kosher salt

fresh black pepper

FOR THE BANANA FAROFA:

2 tablespoons olive oil

¼ cup onions, diced small

1 teaspoon garlic, minced

1 teaspoon kosher salt

1 banana, peeled and diced small

1½ cups coarse manioc flour

1 tablespoon butter

1 tablespoon fresh cilantro, finely chopped

PREP TIME: 10 minutes

TOTAL TIME: 3 hours

YIELD: 8 servings

CHILE PIQUÍN SHORT RIB OVER SWEET CORN TAMAL

INGREDIENTS:

8 Sweet Corn Tamales (see recipe pg. 33)

Chile Piquín Short Rib (see recipe below)

Salsa Criolla (see recipe pg. 99)

Blue Cheese Crema (see recipe pg. 103)

FOR THE CHILE PIQUÍN SHORT RIBS:

3 tablespoons piquín chile powder

1 tablespoon paprika

1 tablespoon ground coriander

1 teaspoon garlic powder

1 teaspoon onion powder

½ tablespoon kosher salt

2 pounds short rib, boneless, cut into 4-ounce pieces

2 tablespoons Worcestershire sauce

2 tablespoons garlic, minced, divided

1¼ cups red wine, divided

2 tablespoons vegetable oil

½ cup red peppers, diced small

¼ cup onions, diced small

2 cups beef or chicken stock

¼ cup maple syrup

2 tablespoons agave syrup

The piquín chile is tiny only in size. In flavor, it's a giant. In this recipe, it revs up fork-tender short ribs. Those slowly braised short ribs make a regal topping for a Sweet Corn Tamal.

1. In a medium-sized bowl, whisk together piquín chile, paprika, coriander, garlic powder, onion powder, and salt.
2. Evenly coat all sides of the short rib with the spice blend. Add Worcestershire sauce, 1 tablespoon minced garlic and ¼ cup of the red wine. Cover and place marinated short ribs in the refrigerator for at least 2 hours or overnight.
3. In a large, deep skillet, heat vegetable oil over medium-high heat. Add short rib pieces to skillet and sear on all sides until browned, about 5 minutes per side.
4. Add red peppers, onions, the remaining 1 tablespoon of minced garlic, the remaining 1 cup of red wine, 2 cups beef or chicken stock, and maple syrup.
5. Bring to a boil then braise, covered, for 2½ hours.
6. Once the short rib is fork tender, remove them from the skillet. Let the sauce cool slightly, then place in a blender. Blend until smooth.
7. Return the sauce to the skillet and bring to a boil. (If using an immersion blender, blend sauce in skillet and bring to a boil.)
8. Add agave syrup and let the sauce reduce by half, about 10 minutes.
9. Return the short rib pieces to the sauce and remove from heat.

COMPOSE THE DISH:

Place a tamal in the center of each plate. Top it with the Chile Piquín Short Rib, then with the Salsa Criolla. Serve tamale dish with a side of Blue Cheese Crema.

BEEF TENDERLOIN TACOS WITH BLUE CHEESE SLAW AND CRISPY ONIONS

PREP TIME: 20 minutes

TOTAL TIME: 30 minutes

YIELD: 4 servings

You may recognize some steak-house flavor notes in this recipe: the grilled tenderloin, the blue cheese in the crispy "salad," even the crispy onion that tops the final dish. This steak is served atop fresh corn tortillas to make a taco that's worthy of any steak house.

1. Prepare a hot charcoal or gas grill. Season the beef liberally on both sides with salt and pepper.
2. Place beef on hot grill and cook without moving until there are grill marks, 4–5 minutes.
3. Turn the meat over and grill for another 2–3 minutes for medium rare, 4 minutes for medium, 5 minutes or longer for medium well.
4. Remove beef from grill and let it rest for at least 3 minutes before slicing.
5. Cut beef tenderloin against the grain into 4-inch-long and ¼-inch-thick slices.

BUILD THE TACO:

Warm the corn tortillas on the grill for 20 seconds. Top the warmed tortillas with the Blue Cheese Slaw, then the sliced Beef Tenderloin. Crown the layers with Crispy Onions. Serve with Salsa Criolla (optional).

INGREDIENTS:

8 Soft Corn Tortillas (see recipe pg. 23)

Blue Cheese Slaw (see recipe pg. 115)

Beef Tenderloin (see recipe below)

Crispy Onions (see recipe pg. 338)

Salsa Criolla (optional; see recipe pg. 99)

FOR THE BEEF TENDERLOIN:

2 pounds beef tenderloin

kosher salt

freshly ground black pepper

CHILES EN NOGADA TACO STYLE

Here's a dish that salutes Mexico not only in flavor profile but also in color. Traditionally, Chiles en Nogada shine in the red, green, and white colors of the Mexican flag. It is a celebrated dish that's popular at Christmastime: roasted chiles stuffed with a nutty, fruity meat filling and topped with a cool and creamy walnut sauce. The sprinkling of pomegranate seeds gives the dish a gorgeous pop of red. In this recipe, we go from tradition to taco by spooning the ingredients atop a sope.

INGREDIENTS:

4 roasted poblano peppers

8 Sopes (see recipe pg. 30)

pomegranate seeds

fresh parsley, chopped

FOR THE FILLING:

2 tablespoons olive oil

1 medium onion, diced small

6 garlic cloves, minced

¼ cup green chiles (Anaheim, California chiles, or poblanos), diced small

1 tablespoon jalapeño, diced small

1 pound ground beef

1 cup tomatoes, diced small

2 tablespoons fresh cilantro, finely chopped

2 tablespoons fresh parsley, finely chopped

1 tablespoon fresh mint, finely chopped

1 teaspoon ancho chile powder

1 teaspoon dried oregano

½ cup dried apricots, diced small

2 tablespoons raisins

½ cup pear, diced small

½ cup red apple, diced small

¼ cup pine nuts, toasted

¼ cup almonds, shaved

¼ cup sweet red wine

2 teaspoons kosher salt

1 teaspoon black pepper

FOR THE WALNUT SAUCE:

1 cup goat cheese

1 cup evaporated milk

½ cup heavy cream

1 cup walnuts

1 teaspoon salt

1 teaspoon white pepper

3 slices of white bread, crust removed

MAKE THE FILLING:

1. In a large skillet, heat olive oil over medium-high heat. Add onions, garlic, green chiles, and jalapeño. Cook for about 2 minutes, until onions become translucent.

2. Add ground beef to skillet, stirring occasionally to evenly brown the beef. After about 3 minutes, stir in the tomatoes, cilantro, parsley, mint, ancho chile powder, and oregano.

(recipe continues)

3. Add the apricots, raisins, pear, apple, pine nuts, almonds, red wine, salt, and pepper. Simmer and stir occasionally for 5–7 minutes, until the meat is cooked, the fruit is softened, and all ingredients are nicely melded.

MAKE THE SAUCE:

1. In a blender, combine goat cheese, evaporated milk, heavy cream, walnuts, salt, and white pepper. Blend ingredients until completely smooth.

2. Add bread slices, one by one, and continue to blend until the sauce is thick and smooth. Set aside.

ASSEMBLE THE DISH:

1. Cut roasted poblano peppers into ¼-inch-thick strips.

2. Place 1 large spoonful of beef filling on each sope, then cover with strips of the poblano peppers.

3. Top with 1 large spoonful of the Walnut Sauce. Garnish with a sprinkling of pomegranate seeds and chopped parsley.

PULLED BEEF AREPAS WITH ONIONS AGRIDOLCE

PREP TIME: 25 minutes

TOTAL TIME: 1 hour and 30 minutes

YIELD: 4 servings

The sweet and sour onions in this arepa dish offer a zesty contrast to the pulled beef. The earthy arepa soaks up all the flavors.

1. Using a sharp knife, split open the still-warm arepas like a pita pocket, making a slit in the top and wiggling a knife into the center of the arepa to create a pocket.
2. Stuff the arepa with the Pulled Beef and top with the Onions Agridolce.

INGREDIENTS:

4 Arepas (see recipe pg. 7)

Pulled Beef (see recipe pg. 247 from Pulled Beef Nachos recipe)

Onions Agridolce (see recipe pg. 100)

PREP TIME: 10 minutes

TOTAL TIME: 20 minutes

YIELD: 4 servings

HERB-CRUSTED LAMB TENDERLOIN

INGREDIENTS:

8 Puffy Tortillas (see recipe pg. 29)

Mint Avocado Pico de Gallo (see recipe pg. 74)

Herb-Crusted Lamb (see recipe below)

1 red jalapeño, shaved, to garnish

FOR THE HERB-CRUSTED LAMB:

1½ tablespoons ground coriander

1 tablespoon fresh cilantro, finely chopped

1 tablespoon fresh mint, finely chopped

1 tablespoon fresh parsley, finely chopped

1 teaspoon fresh thyme leaves

1 teaspoon rosemary, finely chopped

½ tablespoon lemon zest

½ cup almonds, chopped

1 teaspoon chile de arbol powder

kosher salt

1 pound lamb tenderloin, cut into ½-inch-by-2-inch strips

1 tablespoon vegetable oil, plus more for brushing lamb

1 tablespoon Dijon mustard

fresh ground black pepper

Here's my take on the lamb and mint flavor combo: an Herb-Crusted Lamb that gets a kick from Mint Avocado Pico. Pay close attention to the cooking times when searing the lamb, so that it does not overcook.

1. In a medium-size bowl, combine coriander, cilantro, mint, parsley, thyme, rosemary, lemon zest, almonds, chile de arbol, and 1 teaspoon salt.
2. Brush the lamb tenderloin strips lightly with vegetable oil. Brush strips with Dijon mustard and roll them in the herb-almond mixture. (Make sure lamb is covered evenly on all sides by herbs and almonds.) Season with salt and pepper.
3. In a flat-top griddle or flat skillet, heat 1 tablespoon of vegetable oil over medium-high heat.
4. Place lamb on hot griddle and sear for 1 minute and 30 seconds on 1 side. Flip and cook for 1 minute longer or until the lamb is golden brown on all sides. Total cooking time is about 4 minutes.
5. Remove lamb from skillet and let it rest for 5 minutes. When rested, slice the lamb into ½-inch-thick slices.

BUILD THE TACOS:

Spoon the Mint Avocado Pico on top of warm Puffy Tortillas, then top with the Herb-Crusted Lamb slices. Crown with red jalapeño shavings.

PREP TIME: 30 minutes

TOTAL TIME: 35 minutes

YIELD: 4 servings

SPICY STIR-FRY LAMB SOPES

This sake-marinated lamb is quick and delicious when seared in a wok and then stir-fried with hot spices. With a cooling cilantro sauce, it makes a globally inspired topping for sopes.

1. In a medium-size bowl, combine egg white, 2 tablespoons of sake, cornstarch, coriander, salt, and pepper. Add lamb and let it marinate for ½ hour, chilled.

2. Heat a wok or large skillet over high heat. Add 1 tablespoon of the vegetable oil and allow it to heat up. Toss in lamb cubes and stir-fry them for 1 to 2 minutes until they are seared and golden brown. Place lamb in a bowl and set aside.

3. Heat the remaining 1 tablespoon of oil in the skillet or wok. When oil is hot, add coriander seeds, red jalapeño and chile de arbol and stir-fry for 30 seconds.

4. Return the lamb to skillet or wok, add cumin and the remaining ¼ cup sake. Stir-fry for another 2 minutes, then add the red onions and scallions. Sauté for 30 seconds, remove from heat and garnish with chopped mint.

BUILD THE SOPES:

Put Fava Bean Spread on the sopes. Top with the Spicy Stir-Fry Lamb. Serve with a side of Green Cilantro Sauce.

INGREDIENTS:

Fava Bean Spread (see recipe pg. 40)

8 Sopes (see recipe pg. 30)

Spicy Stir-Fry Lamb (see recipe below)

Green Cilantro Sauce (see recipe pg. 49)

FOR THE SPICY STIR-FRY LAMB SOPES:

1 egg white

2 tablespoons, plus ¼ cup sake, divided

3 teaspoons cornstarch

1 teaspoon ground coriander

1 teaspoon salt

½ teaspoon black pepper

1 pound lamb tenderloin, cut into 1-inch cubes

2 tablespoons vegetable oil, divided

1 tablespoon coriander seeds

1 tablespoon red jalapeño, deveined and seeded and thinly sliced

2 tablespoons chile de arbol, thinly sliced

½ tablespoon cumin

½ cup red onion, thinly sliced

4 whole scallions, sliced diagonally

1 tablespoon fresh mint, finely chopped

PREP TIME: 30 minutes

TOTAL TIME: 2 hours

YIELD: 6 servings

BRAISED VEAL SHANK

This is my idea of comfort upon comfort: slow-braised veal draped atop an earthy tamal, then topped with a dollop of Ají Amarillo Crema. Don't toss the marrow bones after the braise— serve them with your tamales for a luxurious touch.

INGREDIENTS:

6 Roasted Red Pepper Tamales (see recipe pg. 34)

Braised Veal Shank (see recipe below)

Ají Amarillo Crema (see recipe pg. 107)

sprig of fresh Italian parsley

Salsa Criolla (see recipe pg. 99)

FOR THE BRAISED VEAL SHANK:

4 veal shanks, bone-in

kosher salt, for seasoning

black pepper, for seasoning

flour, for dusting

2 tablespoons vegetable oil

½ cup carrots, diced small

½ cup celery, diced small

1 cup onion, diced small

2 tablespoons garlic, minced

½ tablespoon red jalapeño, minced

1 cup red wine

1 cup tomato sauce

1 tablespoon basil, finely chopped

1 tablespoon fresh oregano, finely chopped

1 tablespoon sugar

1 cup beef stock

1. Preheat oven to 325F degrees. Season veal shanks on both sides with salt and pepper. Lightly dust each side with flour.
2. In an oven-safe, deep skillet, heat 2 tablespoons of vegetable oil over medium-high heat. Cook veal shanks for 4 minutes on each side and remove them from skillet.
3. Add the carrots, celery, onion, garlic, and red jalapeño to pan, and sauté for 3 minutes.
4. Return veal shanks to the pan and add red wine. Let the wine reduce a bit, then stir in the tomato sauce, basil, oregano, sugar, and beef stock. Bring to a boil. Cover the pan tightly with aluminum foil and place it in the oven for 1½ hours.
5. Remove veal shanks from skillet and slice or pull them apart into ½-inch pieces. Reserve the shank bone with marrow for serving.

BUILD THE TAMALES:

1. Place the Roasted Red Pepper Tamal on the center of a plate and top it with the veal. Add a dollop of the Ají Amarillo Crema on top and garnish with a sprig of Italian parsley.
2. Serve tamal with a marrow bone on the side as well as with a side of the Salsa Criolla.

CHAPTER 12

VEGGIES

There is so much flavor in these veggie "tacos" that they can easily take center-plate role as delicious entrées. You haven't fully explored the potential of an avocado until you've grilled it in its skin and tasted the smoky, creamy result. And you may be surprised to find there could be more to a good Caprese layering than the tomato-mozz-basil routine.

These veggie dishes work hard to showcase one of the central themes of my "New Taco Classics"—build flavor, layer upon layer, for a truly successful dish.

VEGGIE RECIPES

PREP TIME: 5 minutes

TOTAL TIME: 15 minutes

YIELD: 4 servings

WHITE BEAN AND SPINACH TOSTADA

INGREDIENTS:

4 Tostadas (see recipe pg. 25)

White Bean Spread (see recipe pg. 42)

2 cups fresh spinach, thinly sliced

1 avocado, cut in chunks

Spicy Pepper Salsa (see recipe pg. 89)

1 cup Cotija cheese, grated

Chipotle Crema (see recipe pg. 104)

A creamy puree of white beans forms the base of this delicious tostada. The spicy salsa revs up the layering.

1. Spread the top of the tostada with the White Bean Spread. On top of the puree, layer first the spinach, then the avocado, then the Spicy Pepper Salsa.
2. Sprinkle the top layer with Cotija cheese and add a dollop of the Chipotle Crema as a crowning touch.

TOSTONES WITH AVOCADO-ROASTED POBLANO SPREAD

A Tostón dresses up nicely with a creamy, smoky spread of avocado and roasted poblano chiles.

In a mixing bowl, whisk the olive oil, vinegar, salt, and pepper until well combined. Add smashed avocado, onion, cilantro, mayonnaise, chile poblano, and tomato and then mix together until ingredients are well combined into a spread. Fold in remaining diced avocado.

TO ASSEMBLE:

Place the 6 Tostones on a serving platter and spoon the Avocado-Roasted Poblano Spread on top of each one. Sprinkle each with the grated cheese.

PREP TIME: 5 minutes
TOTAL TIME: 15 minutes
YIELD: 6 servings

INGREDIENTS:

6 Tostones (see recipe pg. 315)

2 cups Avocado-Roasted Poblano Spread (recipe below)

1 cup of sharp cheese or mozzarella cheese, grated

FOR THE AVOCADO-ROASTED POBLANO SPREAD:

1 tablespoon extra-virgin olive oil

½ teaspoon white vinegar

½ teaspoon kosher salt

¼ teaspoon black pepper

1 Hass avocado, cut in half (one half smashed, the other half diced small)

¼ cup red onion, diced small

1 tablespoon cilantro, finely chopped

2 tablespoons mayonnaise

1 chile poblano, (roasted, seeded and skin off), diced small

1 tomato, diced small

PREP TIME: 20 minutes

TOTAL TIME: 25 minutes

YIELD: 6 servings

AREPA CAPRESE

INGREDIENTS:

4 fried Arepas (see recipe on pg. 7)

vegetable oil

1 yellow tomato, cut in 6 slices

kosher salt

pepper, to taste

2 cups baby arugula

1 large fresh Mozzarella di Bufala ball, cut in 6 slices

Basil-Spinach Crema (see recipe pg. 106)

Call this dish an Italian and Venezuelan romance, the pairing of a tomato-mozzarella salad with a warm arepa. It's wedded bliss.

FRY THE AREPA:

In a fryer, heat vegetable oil to 350F degrees. Fry each arepa for 2½ minutes on each side or until golden brown. Remove and place on paper towels to drain.

ASSEMBLE THE DISH:

1. Season the tomato slices with salt and pepper.
2. Slice the arepa and fill it with the baby arugula, yellow tomato slice, and fresh mozzarella slice. Add a drizzle of Basil-Spinach Crema on top of the fillings.

PREP TIME: 10 minutes

TOTAL TIME: 20 minutes

YIELD: 4 servings

GRILLED AVOCADO TACOS

What make these tacos extra special are the smoky notes offered by the grilled avocado. Those smoky notes are amplified by a poblano-laced pico.

PREPARE THE GRILLED AVOCADO:

1. In a small bowl, whisk together the olive oil, lemon juice, chile de arbol, salt, and pepper.
2. Brush the avocado slices with oil mixture and place them on a very hot grill or grill pan. Sear all sides of the avocado slices.
3. Remove slices from grill and season them with salt. Carefully remove the skin of the avocado.

BUILD THE TACOS:

Top each Puffy Tortilla with Corn Poblano Pico de Gallo, Cilantro Crema, and half a Grilled Avocado in slices.

INGREDIENTS:

4 Puffy Tortillas (see recipe pg. 29)

Corn Poblano Pico de Gallo (see recipe pg. 73)

Cilantro Crema (see recipe pg. 110)

2 Grilled Avocados (recipe below)

FOR THE GRILLED AVOCADO:

¼ cup olive oil

juice of 1 lemon

1 teaspoon chile de arbol powder

kosher salt

pepper, to taste

2 avocados, cut in slices with skin on

PREP TIME: 5 minutes
TOTAL TIME: 35 minutes
YIELD: 4 servings

INGREDIENTS:

8 Tostadas (see recipe pg. 25)

Roasted Garlic Crema (see recipe pg. 109)

Herb-Roasted Beets and Potatoes (recipe below)

¼ cup crumbled goat cheese

Candied Pecans (recipe below)

FOR THE HERB-ROASTED BEETS AND POTATOES:

8 cups of water

1½ cups red beets, cut into ½-inch cubes

1½ cups golden beets, cut into ½-inch cubes

1 cup baby red potatoes, boiled and halved

¼ cup olive oil

¼ cup fresh parsley, finely chopped

1 tablespoon fresh thyme, finely chopped

1 teaspoon fresh rosemary, finely chopped

1 teaspoon kosher salt

1 tablespoon aged balsamic vinegar

FOR THE CANDIED PECANS:

¼ cup chicken stock

1 tablespoon fresh lemon juice

3 tablespoons sugar

½ cup pecans

ROASTED BEETS AND POTATO TOSTADA

Red and yellow beets, along with potatoes, star in an herby, roasted topping for crispy tostadas. The sweet finale: delicious candied pecans.

1. Preheat oven to 400F degrees.
2. In two saucepans each filled with 4 cups of water, boil red and golden beets separately for 20 minutes. Strain beets and place them in a medium-size bowl.
3. Add the potatoes and olive oil to bowl. Fold in the parsley, thyme, rosemary, salt, and balsamic vinegar. Gently toss ingredients to coat.
4. Place beets and potatoes on a sheet pan and roast them in the oven for 15 minutes. Remove from oven and season with salt.

MAKE THE CANDIED PECANS:

1. Pour chicken stock into a small skillet set over high heat. Add lemon juice, sugar, and pecans and bring to a boil.
2. Continue to cook, stirring often, until the liquid is evaporated and the pecans have caramelized and are sticky, 3 to 4 minutes.
3. Immediately scrape the pecans onto a parchment-paper-lined plate. Set aside to cool completely, about 20 minutes.

BUILD THE TOSTADAS:

Spread each tostada with the Roasted Garlic Crema. Top with the beets and potatoes and crumbled goat cheese. Sprinkle the pecans on top.

BUTTER LETTUCE JÍCAMA TACOS

PREP TIME: 10 minutes
TOTAL TIME: 15 minutes
YIELD: 6–8 servings

These tacos are fresh all the way around, from the butter lettuce wrapping to the crisp jícama to the zesty orange. There are so many layers of flavors in this dish, you'll crave it year-round.

1. In a small bowl, make vinaigrette by whisking together 2 tablespoons of the orange juice, coconut vinegar, chipotle adobo, agave, lemon juice, and olive oil.
2. Toss jícama and chayote with vinaigrette. Season with salt and pepper.
3. Spoon about ⅓ cup jícama-chayote mixture into the center of each Boston lettuce leaf.
4. Divide orange pieces among the lettuce leaf tacos. Sprinkle Cotija cheese and pomegranate seeds evenly over each taco.

INGREDIENTS:

Orange-Chipotle Vinaigrette (see recipe below)

2 cups jícama, grated

½ cup chayote, grated

kosher salt

fresh ground pepper

6–8 Boston lettuce leaves

1 whole orange, segmented, with each segment cut in thirds

¼ cup Cotija cheese, crumbled

¼ cup pomegranate seeds

FOR THE VINAIGRETTE:

juice of 1 whole orange

1 tablespoon coconut vinegar

1 tablespoon chipotle adobo

1 tablespoon agave syrup

1 tablespoon lemon juice

¼ cup olive oil

PREP TIME: 10 minutes

TOTAL TIME: 15 minutes

YIELD: 6 servings

GUAYANÉS CHEESE CACHAPAS

Venezuelan-style Guayanés cheese is a fresh, soft white cheese that makes a delicious topping for arepas and cachapas. In this recipe, I pair it with an avocado-rich Guasacaca sauce.

INGREDIENTS:

6 Sweet Corn Cakes (see recipe below)

1½ cups Guayanés cheese, cut in chunks

Guasacaca (see recipe pg. 90)

FOR THE SWEET CORN CAKES:

1 cup of corn (fresh sweet corn kernels)

½ cup of queso blanco

½ cup of precooked corn flour (sweet)

1 tablespoon butter, unsalted

2 tablespoons milk

1 teaspoon kosher salt

1 tablespoon sugar

2 tablespoons all-purpose flour

1 egg

MAKE SWEET CORN CAKES:

1. In a food processor, add all of the ingredients and process until a loose dough forms, about 30 seconds. Let dough rest for a few minutes.
2. Preheat a greased flat-top grill or skillet over medium heat. Ladle 2 tablespoons of the corn mixture onto the hot skillet and cook the corn cakes for 3 minutes on each side. Set aside.

BUILD THE DISH:

Top the corn cakes with the cheese chunks and drizzle each cake with Guasacaca sauce.

NEW TACO CLASSICS

THE SIDES

CHAPTER 13

SIDES

An extraordinary taco deserves a great side dish. And I don't mean a scoop of plain refried beans. I mean a creamy Peruvian corn gratin, a flavorful succotash with a trio of beans, a hearty queso fundido, and an assortment of crispy delicacies.

In this chapter, we'll give a traditionally Southern Hoppin' John a new name and a Latin accent. We'll grill the most deliciously seasoned corn. We'll learn to make fries and croutons out of avocados. And we'll top the sweetest of plantains with the tangiest of pickled onions. Plus, I'll share my tip for an ingenious yet simple way to extract maximum flavor from a simple lemon or lime.

SIDES RECIPES

PREP TIME: 10 minutes

COOK TIME: 6–8 minutes

TOTAL TIME: 16–18 minutes

YIELD: 6 servings

GRILLED CORN

Grilled corn on the cob is proof that street food is some of the best food in the world. For an added rustic touch—and grilling convenience—I make a handle out of the corn husk as I grill the cob.

1. Prepare a hot charcoal or gas grill. Pull back husk from corn cob, but do not remove it. Remove corn silk.
2. Tie up loose husk with a string of the same husk, making a handle (away from the corn cob).
3. In a medium-size bowl, whisk together butter, salt, chile de arbol, ají amarillo, and lemon juice. Set aside.
4. Holding corn by your makeshift handle, place the cob on the hot grill, turning the cob occasionally to ensure all sides cook evenly.
5. Once grill marks appear, brush butter mixture on corn cob and continue to apply butter to coat all sides as you turn the cob. After 6–8 minutes, remove corn from grill and brush liberally with butter.
6. Arrange buttered corn on a plate. Drizzle Chile-Lime Crema on top. Sprinkle with Cotija cheese and a pinch of ground chile de arbol.

INGREDIENTS:

6 whole corn cobs, in husk

½ cup unsalted butter, room temperature

2 teaspoons kosher salt

1 teaspoon ground chile de arbol, plus a pinch for each corn cob (for garnish)

2 teaspoons ají amarillo powder

1 tablespoon lemon juice

¼ cup Chile-Lime Crema (see recipe pg. 110)

½ cup Cotija cheese, crumbled

FIDEOS RICE

PREP TIME: 5 minutes

COOK TIME: 25–26 minutes

TOTAL TIME: 30–31 minutes

YIELD: 4 servings

The secret to this rice pilaf is to toast the pasta strands as well as the rice in the pan before adding water. This produces fluffier rice that doesn't clump.

1. In a large, deep skillet or pot, toast the pasta until the strands are golden brown, without burning. When the pasta is toasted, remove it from the skillet.
2. Add the olive oil, garlic, and rice to the pan. Sauté for about 5–6 minutes.
3. Add the water, salt, and toasted angel hair pasta, stir and cover. Cook over low heat for about 20 minutes until tender.
4. Turn the heat off. With a fork, fluff the rice and fold in the almonds.

INGREDIENTS:

½ cup of angel hair pasta

2 tablespoons olive oil

1 tablespoons garlic paste

1 cup basmati rice

1 cup of water

½ tablespoon kosher salt

½ cup of sliced almonds

PREP TIME: 5 minutes

COOK TIME: 15 minutes

TOTAL TIME: 20 minutes

YIELD: 6 servings

BLACK BEAN SUCCOTASH

Three types of beans give this succotash contrast and color. Herbs, aromatics, and baby bell peppers make it sing.

INGREDIENTS:

¼ cup olive oil

3 tablespoons unsalted butter

2 whole garlic cloves, minced

1 medium onion, diced small

1 cup baby bell peppers (assorted colors), diced small

2 cups black beans, cooked and rinsed

1 cup frozen black-eyed peas, rinsed and drained

1 cup frozen lima beans, rinsed and drained

2 cups fresh or frozen corn kernels

kosher salt

fresh ground black pepper

¼ cup dry white wine

1 tablespoon fresh cilantro, coarsely chopped

1 tablespoon fresh thyme leaves

1. In a large skillet, heat oil and butter over medium-high heat.
2. Add garlic and onion; cook until translucent, about 4 minutes. Add bell peppers, black beans, black-eyed peas, lima beans, and corn. Season with salt and pepper. Cook for 5 minutes.
3. Add white wine. Cook until vegetables are tender, stirring occasionally, about 5 minutes. Remove from heat, stir in herbs and serve.

BLACK BEANS WITH QUESO FUNDIDO

The key to presenting this queso dish is to make sure to warm the serving plate, bowl, or platter. This recipe works with any type of beans or melting cheeses. Cheddar, mozzarella, or Monterey Jack all work extremely well. I like serving the Black Beans with Queso in a nice cast-iron skillet or a clay pot that can be warmed on top of a stove, but any nonstick skillet will work.

1. Warm an oven-safe serving dish or bowl in the oven or on the stove.
2. In a large skillet, heat oil over medium-high heat. Sauté onions and garlic for about 1 minute. Add jalapeño, black beans, cumin, oregano, and salt and cook for about 5 minutes.
3. Place beans in warmed serving dish. Top the beans with 3 cups of shredded cheese, making sure to evenly cover all the beans, about 1 inch thick.
4. Cover dish with aluminum foil and bake on low heat for at least 20 minutes or until cheese has melted completely.

PREP TIME: 5 minutes

COOK TIME: 10 minutes

TOTAL TIME: 15 minutes

YIELD: 6 servings

INGREDIENTS:

2 tablespoons vegetable or olive oil

½ cup onions, diced small

1 tablespoon garlic, minced

1 tablespoon jalapeño, minced

2 cups black beans, cooked

1 teaspoon cumin

1 teaspoon dried oregano

1 teaspoon kosher salt

3 cups shredded cheese, Mexican blend or cheddar

PREP TIME: 10 minutes

COOK TIME: 1 hour

YIELD: 6 servings

BLACK-EYED PEAS GUISO

INGREDIENTS:

½ cup vegetable oil

2 cups dry cured meat (carne seca), diced and soaked overnight

1 cup white onion, diced small

½ cup carrots, diced small

½ cup celery, diced small

2 tablespoons garlic, minced

1 tablespoon red jalapeño, diced small

1 tablespoon cumin

½ tablespoon paprika

½ tablespoon dried oregano

½ tablespoon ground ginger

1 teaspoon dried rosemary

1 pound black-eyed peas, frozen

5 cups water

1 smoked ham hock

¼ cup fresh cilantro, finely chopped

This dish is inspired by a classic Brazilian feijoada, although we are using black-eyed peas instead of the traditional black beans. I wanted to lighten up the recipe, so I cut back on the fatty meats that typically go into a feijoada. But we didn't cut back on flavor—this guiso (stew) is brimming with spices and smoky notes from the ham hock and carne seca.

1. In a large, deep skillet, heat vegetable oil over medium-high heat.
2. Add dried meat and cook for 1 minute. Stir in onions, carrots, celery, garlic, and red jalapeño. Cook for 2 minutes.
3. Add cumin, paprika, dried oregano, ground ginger, and rosemary and continue to cook for an additional 2 minutes.
4. Add the black-eyed peas, water, and ham hock and bring to a boil. Reduce heat to medium low, cover, and simmer for 45 minutes to 1 hour.
5. Remove ham hock from pan, then remove pan from heat. Garnish black-eyed peas with cilantro.

HOPPIN' JOSÉ RICE

PREP TIME: 5 minutes
COOK TIME: 15 minutes
TOTAL TIME: 20 minutes
YIELD: 4 servings

The American South loves its Hoppin' John, especially around New Year's. It represents luck and prosperity. This is my version of this traditional rice using my recipe for Black-Eyed Peas Guiso (stew) and lima beans. This is a great way to enhance your leftover rice. To make it even better, toast the rice a bit to create a crust on the finished rice dish.

INGREDIENTS:

2 tablespoons vegetable oil

½ cup bacon, diced

¾ cup lima beans, thawed

¾ cup Black-Eyed Peas Guiso (see recipe pg. 308)

2 cups cooked white rice

olive oil, to drizzle

2 tablespoons fresh cilantro, finely chopped

1. In a large, deep skillet, heat vegetable oil over medium-high heat. Add bacon and cook for 3 minutes to render fat.
2. Add lima beans and Black-Eyed Peas Guiso. Cook for 2 minutes, then add cooked rice. Let rice and beans cook on medium heat to toast rice about 10 minutes.
3. Remove pan from heat and spoon Hoppin' José onto a serving plate. Drizzle with olive oil and garnish with cilantro.

PREP TIME: 5 minutes

COOK TIME: 5 minutes

TOTAL TIME: 10 minutes

YIELD: 4 servings

INGREDIENTS:

4 whole green plantains, large, skin on

vegetable oil for frying

kosher salt

MARIQUITAS

These plantain chips make a stellar snack or side for tacos and sandwiches. I don't even bother to remove the peel—I slice them thin and fry them hot, and they're delicious.

1. Slice the plantains lengthwise, with the peel on, using a mandolin or vegetable slicer, ⅟₁₆ of an inch thick.
2. In a large skillet, heat oil to 350F degrees. (Oil should fill a third of the skillet.)
3. Add plantain slices to hot oil and fry for 5 minutes until crispy and golden brown.
4. Remove Mariquitas with slotted spoon and allow them to drain on paper towels for a few minutes. Season generously with salt and serve hot.

PREP TIME: 5 minutes
COOK TIME: 20 minutes
TOTAL TIME: 25 minutes
YIELD: 4 servings

TOSTONES

These twice-fried green plantains are not only crispy—they're extra flavorful. The secret: a dipping solution of salted water, lemon juice, and garlic. I dip the plantains in this water and pat them dry before their second frying.

INGREDIENTS:

2 cups water

2 tablespoons kosher salt

juice of 1 lemon

3 whole garlic cloves, minced

vegetable oil for frying

2 whole green plantains, peeled and cut in half

1. In a medium-size bowl, whisk together water, salt, lemon juice, and garlic for 1 minute until salt dissolves. Set aside.
2. Heat the oil in a large skillet over high heat until it reaches 350F degrees. (Oil should fill a third of the skillet.)
3. Add plantain halves to oil and cook for three minutes.
4. Remove plantains with slotted spoon and allow them to drain on paper towels for a few minutes.
5. Dip plantains into water-lemon-garlic mixture for 20 seconds. Remove the plantains from the mixture and pat dry with paper towels.
6. Using a plantain press or the back of a flat plate, smash plantains to ¼ of an inch thick and 4–5 inches in diameter.
7. Return the smashed plantains to hot oil (350F degrees) and fry them until golden brown, 4–5 minutes, depending on the thickness of the plantain.
8. Remove the Tostones with a slotted spoon. Allow them to drain on paper towels. While they're hot, season them generously with kosher salt.

PREP TIME: 5 minutes

COOK TIME: 25 minutes

TOTAL TIME: 30 minutes

YIELD: 4 servings

INGREDIENTS:

2 tablespoons olive oil

1 tablespoon garlic paste or minced

1 cup brown rice

½ tablespoon kosher salt

2½ cups water

⅓ cup bacon, fat rendered crispy and cubed (or ham)

⅓ cup onion, diced small

⅓ cup leeks, diced small

⅓ cup celery, diced small

⅓ cup cilantro, finely chopped

⅓ cup parsley, finely chopped

⅔ cup sweet peppers, diced small (1 each red, orange, yellow)

1 tablespoon raisins

⅓ cup sweet corn kernels

⅓ cup sliced almonds

freshly ground black pepper, to taste

VEGETABLE MEDLEY RICE

Adding aromatics, crisp bacon, corn, peppers and raisins after this rice has cooked gives the finished dish the look and texture of a true medley.

1. In a pot over medium-high heat, add the olive oil, garlic, rice, and salt. Sauté the rice for 5 minutes. Add the water and bring to a boil. Once boiling, cover and reduce heat to low. Cook for 20 minutes until tender.
2. With a fork fluff the rice. Add the remaining ingredients, and adjust the salt and pepper to taste. Toss well to incorporate the ingredients.

GRILLED AVOCADO SALAD

PREP TIME: 10 minutes
COOK TIME: 20 minutes
TOTAL TIME: 30 minutes
YIELD: 4 servings

When grilling soft-flesh fruits or vegetables, like avocado or peaches, it's always a good idea to keep the skin on to help keep the flesh intact. For this salad, I wanted to give a smoky flavor to the avocado, hearts of palm and corn by charring them first. You can use a simple grill pan to achieve this—and one made of cast iron is even better.

1. In a small bowl, whisk together olive oil, lemon juice, salt, pepper, and chile de arbol.
2. Combine oil and butter, to brush on ingredients. Brush corn, avocado, and hearts of palm with oil-butter mixture and place on very hot grill or grill pan. Rotate them, basting occasionally, to achieve a nice brown char. Remove from grill and season with salt.
3. Prep the veggies: Toss the Napa cabbage and spinach with 1 tablespoon of the Orange-Chipotle Vinaigrette. Slice hearts of palm in ½-inch pieces. Remove avocado from skin. With a knife, cut kernels from corn.
4. Arrange on a serving plate: First place the cabbage and spinach mix in center. Top with hearts of palm, avocado and corn kernels.
5. Squeeze the half lemon over salad. Garnish with red onions and radish slices. Drizzle the remaining tablespoon of Orange-Chipotle Vinaigrette over salad and serve.

INGREDIENTS:

¼ cup olive oil, plus 3 tablespoons for brushing

juice of 1 lemon, plus ½ lemon for finishing

kosher salt

freshly ground black pepper

1 teaspoon ground chile de arbol

¼ cup melted butter, for brushing

1 whole corn on the cob

1 avocado, ½-inch slices with skin on

4 hearts of palm, halved lengthwise

1 cup Napa cabbage, thinly sliced

1 cup spinach, thinly sliced

2 tablespoons Orange-Chipotle Vinaigrette, divided (see recipe pg. 293)

1 red onion, thinly sliced

1 radish, thinly sliced

PREP TIME: 1 hour

COOK TIME: 5 minutes

TOTAL TIME: 1 hour 5 minutes

YIELD: 4 servings

INGREDIENTS:

¾ cup red onions, thinly sliced

¼ cup red wine vinegar

1 tablespoon agave syrup

2 tablespoons olive oil

1 tablespoon fresh cilantro, finely chopped

kosher salt

black pepper

2 ripe plantains (peel should be black)

vegetable oil (½ inch in the pan)

Pickled Onions (see recipe pg. 97)

SWEET PLANTAINS WITH PICKLED ONIONS

Sweet plantains are a versatile staple in Latin America and the Caribbean. You can bake, steam, boil, or fry them. I love to roast or steam the sweetest plantain in its skin and top it with contrasting flavor notes. Something as simple as pickled onion really can elevate this simple dish.

1. In a small bowl, whisk together onions, vinegar, agave, olive oil, and cilantro, and season with salt and pepper. Set aside at room temperature for 1 hour.
2. Peel the plantains and cut them in half. Then slice each piece in quarters lengthwise.
3. Heat a sauté pan filled ½ inch high with vegetable oil over medium-high heat. Place plantains in small batches in hot oil and fry for 1½–2 minutes on each side, until they are golden brown.
4. Remove plantains from oil and place on paper towels to drain. Season them immediately with salt and pepper.
5. Create a tower with the plantain strips, 3 per row. Crown with Pickled Onions and serve.

PERUVIAN CORN GRATIN

Peruvian corn is one of my favorite ingredients—I absolutely love it. I just had to feature it in this book, as corn is the common ingredient in these pages. The kernel size and texture work so well in a creamy gratinado (or gratin) that's topped with a delicious, golden crust. If you can't find Peruvian corn, you can use fresh white corn kernels in this recipe.

PREP TIME: 10 minutes
COOK TIME: 30 minutes
TOTAL TIME: 40 minutes
YIELD: 4 servings

INGREDIENTS:

1 cup grated Parmigiano Reggiano

¼ cup panko crumbs

2 tablespoons olive oil

½ cup shallots, minced

1 teaspoon garlic, minced

4 cups Peruvian corn (or white corn)

1½ teaspoons kosher salt

⅓ cup white wine

½ cup mascarpone cheese

½ cup heavy cream

1 cup (packed) fresh spinach, chopped

1 teaspoon white pepper

zest of 1 lemon

1 teaspoon lemon juice

1 cup hearts of palm, cut into ½-inch rounds

1. In a small bowl, toss together the Parmigiano Reggiano and panko crumbs, and set aside.
2. Preheat oven to 350F degrees. In an oven-safe skillet, heat oil over medium heat. Add shallots and garlic to hot oil and sauté for 1 minute.
3. Add Peruvian corn and salt. Cook for 4 minutes, then add white wine.
4. Reduce heat to low and add mascarpone cheese and heavy cream. Toss in the spinach, white pepper, lemon zest, lemon juice, and hearts of palm. Stir together and simmer for 2 minutes.
5. Remove pan from heat and sprinkle with cheese-panko mixture. Place skillet in oven and bake for 20 minutes until the cheese is golden brown.

PREP TIME: 5 minutes

COOK TIME: 5 minutes

TOTAL TIME: 10 minutes

YIELD: 4 servings

INGREDIENTS:

1 bag of your favorite tortilla chips

Salsa Verde Cruda (recipe follows)

MOLCAJETE SAUCE: SALSA VERDE CRUDA

2 tomatillos

½ green jalapeño pepper

2 teaspoons kosher salt

3 sprigs cilantro, plus chopped cilantro for garnish

1 tablespoon shallots, minced, to garnish

CHIPS AND SALSA

The molcajete (mortar and pestle) is the magic tool that turns a couple of tomatillos and half a jalapeño into a sauce so delicious it elevates the chips-and-salsa routine. You can use your blender as well, but to extract maximum flavor out of these few ingredients, muddle them well with a pestle.

BEFORE YOU START:

1. Boil tomatillos in water for 5 minutes. Let cool and reserve in water.
2. Boil jalapeño in water for 5 minutes. Let cool. Remove seeds.

MOLCAJETE METHOD:

1. In a molcajete (mortar and pestle), place tomatillos, jalapeño, and salt.
2. Use pestle to muddle ingredients into a sauce. Add cilantro and combine well.
3. To serve, garnish with shallots and chopped cilantro. Serve the sauce with a side of chips.

BLENDER METHOD:

In a blender, mix tomatillos, jalapeño, and salt on medium speed until ingredients are well combined. Add cilantro and blend for another 10 seconds. To serve, garnish with shallots and chopped cilantro. Serve the sauce with a side of chips.

HERBED RICE

Infused with loads of fresh herbs and aromatics and crowned with a fried egg and substantial cheese croutons, this rice teeters on entrée status. It is as fragrant as it is delicious. It's a recipe inspired by a reality we all share from time to time: What do we make for dinner when the fridge and pantry offer few options and we don't feel like going out? Rice and eggs often become our salvation. This is my version of homey rice-and-eggs. It's simple and delicious.

MAKE THE CROUTONS:

In a nonstick pan over medium heat, place cheese cubes and sear on all sides until golden brown. About 30 seconds on each side. Set aside.

MAKE THE RICE:

1. In a large skillet, heat olive oil on medium-high heat. Sauté garlic for 30 seconds. Add scallions and rice and cook for 5 minutes.
2. Add herbs, salt, pepper, and butter. Stir together and cook for another minute.
3. To serve, spoon rice onto serving platter, top with sunny-side-up egg and Cheese Croutons.

PREP TIME: 5 minutes

COOK TIME: 6 minutes

TOTAL TIME: 11 minutes

YIELD: 4 servings

INGREDIENTS:

Cheese Croutons (see recipe pg. 334)

FOR THE CHEESE CROUTONS:

One 10-ounce package "queso para freír" (frying cheese), cut into ½-inch cubes

FOR THE HERBED RICE:

2 tablespoons olive oil

3 cloves garlic, minced

¼ cup scallions, thinly sliced

2 cups cooked rice

½ cup fresh cilantro, finely chopped

½ cup fresh parsley, finely chopped

½ teaspoon fresh rosemary, finely chopped

1 teaspoon thyme, finely chopped

kosher salt

freshly ground black pepper

1 tablespoon butter

1 sunny-side-up egg

PREP TIME: 5 minutes

COOK TIME: 45 minutes

TOTAL TIME: 50 minutes

YIELD: 6 servings

ROASTED SWEET POTATOES WITH CHILE, LIME, AND AGAVE

INGREDIENTS:

2 pounds baby yams, cut in half

¼ cup extra-virgin olive oil

½ tablespoon chile powder

3 tablespoons lime juice

3 tablespoons agave syrup

1 teaspoon kosher salt

1 teaspoon black pepper

Chile powder gives this yam roast a nice kick of heat, while agave syrup lends a sweet note.

1. Preheat oven at 400F degrees.
2. In a large mixing bowl, toss together baby yams with the rest of the ingredients.
3. Spread yam mix on a rimmed baking sheet. Roast for about 45 minutes, until the yams are softened and golden brown. Adjust the salt and pepper, to taste. Serve while hot.

GRILLED CAULIFLOWER WITH HERB DRIZZLE

PREP TIME: 10 minutes

COOK TIME: 8 minutes

TOTAL TIME: 18 minutes

YIELD: 4 servings

In this recipe, meaty cauliflower florets are grilled until golden brown, then tossed with a fragrant sauce of chopped mint, thyme, cilantro, and parsley for a simply beautiful result.

1. Preheat the grill on high. In a bowl, toss the cauliflower florets with olive oil, salt, fresh ground pepper and half of the lemon juice.
2. Grill seasoned florets for about 4 minutes per side, until golden brown.
3. Make the herb sauce: In the same floret seasoning bowl, add the remaining half of the lemon juice (about 1 teaspoon), olive oil, lemon zest, chopped herbs, salt, and pepper. Stir until well combined.
4. Add the grilled cauliflower florets and toss until they are well-coated with the herb sauce. Serve immediately.

INGREDIENTS:

1 head of cauliflower cut into florets, about 20 pieces

2 tablespoons extra-virgin olive oil

1 teaspoon kosher salt

½ teaspoon freshly ground black pepper

juice of 1 lemon, divided

HERB SAUCE:

¼ cup extra-virgin olive oil

zest of 1 lemon

I teaspoon fresh mint, finely chopped

¼ teaspoon thyme, finely chopped

1 tablespoon cilantro, finely chopped

1 tablespoon flat-leaf parsley, finely chopped

pinch of kosher salt

pinch of pepper

TOTAL TIME: 5 minutes

YIELD: 6 servings

INGREDIENTS:

1 tablespoon kosher salt

1 tablespoon ancho powder, chile piquín powder, paprika, or chili powder

2 lemons, cut in half

2 limes, cut in half

2 Meyer lemons, cut in half

SEASONED LEMONS AND LIMES

The genius thing about these chile-seasoned lemons and limes is that, when squeezed, they carry the flavors of the chile salt. Squeeze them on a few avocado slices and taste for yourself how the chile-spiked juice flavors the avocado.

1. In a small mixing bowl, whisk together the salt and ancho (or other chile) powder until well combined.
2. Dip the lemon or lime halves into the seasoned salt. They are now ready to be squeezed onto your favorite dish.

PREP TIME: 5 minutes

COOK TIME: 5 minutes

TOTAL TIME: 10 minutes

YIELD: 4 servings

CHEESE CROUTONS

These crispy-rich croutons add a salty topping to your taco dishes.

INGREDIENTS:

1 cup hard white cheese for frying ("queso para freir"), cut into 1-inch cubes

1 cup rice flour

1 tablespoon chile piquín

½ tablespoon of kosher salt

1. Toss cheese cubes in rice flour, shake to remove excess.
2. Fry them at 350F degrees for 5 minutes. Remove from oil and place on paper towels to drain. Season immediately with chile piquín and salt.

AVOCADO CROUTONS

Avocado cubes make delicious "croutons"—crispy outside and downright luxurious inside.

1. In a skillet, heat oil over medium-high heat.
2. To bread the avocado cubes, toss them first in the rice flour, then in the eggs, then in the panko crumbs.
3. Fry cubes in oil until golden brown on all sides.
4. Remove from oil, place on paper towels to drain and season with ancho chile powder and salt.
5. Squeeze lime over cubes when ready to serve.

PREP TIME: 5 minutes

COOK TIME: 5 minutes

TOTAL TIME: 10 minutes

YIELD: 4 servings

INGREDIENTS:

vegetable oil for frying

1 avocado, peeled and cut into 1-inch cubes

2 cups rice flour

2 eggs, beaten

2 cups panko bread crumbs

1 tablespoon ancho chile powder

kosher salt

1 lime

PREP TIME: 10 minutes

COOK TIME: 5 minutes

TOTAL TIME: 15 minutes

YIELD: 4 servings

AVOCADO FRIES

These spicy fries stand in perfectly for traditional French fries. The avocado holds up really well when fried. The result is a great contrast of creamy and crispy. They go well with a variety of dipping sauces, like the Cilantro Crema in this recipe.

INGREDIENTS:

1 tablespoon chile piquín, plus more for dipping salt

½ tablespoon kosher salt, plus more for dipping salt

1 whole avocado, peeled and cut into 1-inch wedges

I cup rice flour

vegetable oil, for frying

2 limes, cut in half

Cilantro Crema (see recipe pg. 110)

1. Combine chile piquín and salt.
2. Toss avocado wedges in rice flour, shake lightly to remove excess.
3. Fry avocados in vegetable oil (350F degrees) for 5 minutes.
4. Remove from oil, place on paper towels to drain and season with chile piquín and salt.
5. Dip lime halves into chile piquín and salt mixture. Squeeze the dipped lime over the Avocado Fries when ready to eat. Serve with a side of Cilantro Crema.

PREP TIME: 15 minutes

COOK TIME: 3–4 minutes

TOTAL TIME: 20 minutes

YIELD: 8 servings

CRISPY ONIONS

INGREDIENTS:

2 large yellow onions, thinly sliced

2 cups buttermilk

4 cups all-purpose flour

1 tablespoon paprika

1 tablespoon cayenne pepper

1 tablespoon onion powder

1 tablespoon kosher salt

1 tablespoon black pepper

vegetable oil for frying

These slivered onions get a bath in a buttermilk marinade before they are dusted in seasoned flour and fried crispy.

1. In a medium-size bowl, place onions in buttermilk and set aside for 1 hour.
2. In another bowl, whisk together the flour, paprika, cayenne, onion powder, salt, and pepper.
3. Strain onions from buttermilk and toss them in the seasoned flour until they are evenly coated. Shake off excess flour.
4. In a large, deep skillet or fryer, heat oil to 350F degrees. Carefully drop the onions, in small batches, into the oil, using a slotted spoon to separate them. Fry for 3–4 minutes, until golden brown, and remove them with a slotted spoon.
5. Place crispy onions on paper towels to absorb excess oil. Season immediately with salt.

PREP TIME: 15 minutes

COOK TIME: 3-4 minutes

TOTAL TIME: 18-19 minutes

YIELD: 8 servings

CRISPY SHALLOTS

INGREDIENTS:

vegetable oil for frying

4 large shallots, thinly sliced

kosher salt

Pungent and crispy, these shallots make a terrific topping for your favorite tacos.

1. In a large, deep skillet or fryer, heat oil to 275F degrees.
2. Carefully drop shallots into the hot oil, using a slotted spoon to separate them. Fry for 3–4 minutes, until they are golden brown.
3. Remove shallots from the oil with a slotted spoon and place them on paper towels to drain. Immediately season them with salt.

I always say that I have the best job in the world because I do what I am passionate about, what I absolutely love, and that is to cook, talk, teach, and live food 24/7. I couldn't do what I do without the help and support of the people around me. First and foremost, I thank God for giving me so many blessings through-out my life. To my mother, Blanca (for her support in every step of the way throughout this process), to whom I owe everything, thank you for giving me the foundation of love and values that is the glue that holds everything else in place.

To my friends and family, thank you for being by my side and understanding that there is such a thing as unconditional love.

To my absolutely wonderful team: Randy Jackson and Harriet Sternberg, my managers, who are such a wonderful blessing in my life and always keep my best interest at heart; and Natalie Perez, who keeps me organized and shares my vision and goals. Thank you to my agents at William Morris Endeavor Entertain-ment: Sean Perry, Eric Rovner, Amir Shahkhalili, Miles Gidaly and everyone who works so tirelessly to help me reach out to an ever-widening audience. And a big thanks to my staff, Fabian Ospina and Gau-delia Escalona, who worked so intensely on this book and helped me make it a reality.

To my dear friends Joy Mangano and Christie Miranne, I thank you for your wisdom and the opportunity to share with the world what I do and for your sage advice. Thank you to Art Smith for your unconditional brotherly love and for showing me the very best of Southern cuisine. To Jaime Martín del Campo and Ramiro Arvizu for your friendship, support and unparalleled knowledge of Mexican cuisine.

To my best friends, Juan Carlos Ruiz and Flavio Datorre, thanks for staying close to me throughout all these years and for being the best recipe tasters. To my beloved Natalia Datorre, thank you for your unconditional love and support and for helping me make my dreams and this special cookbook come true.

I worked with so many people to bring this book to life. Raymond Garcia, my editor in chief at Celebra, believed in my vision and who I am, not just as a chef but also as a person. To Kim Suarez, Tracy Bernstein and Kiovangie Herrera, thank you for helping me create a voice that is true to myself. To Liz Balmaseda, thank you for putting into written words what I can only say. Thank you to Front of the House, Ann Saks and Ingenious Designs for sharing your beautiful pieces. To Lazara "Lady" Pinon and Claudia Pascual, my glam team, for always making me look my best.

Thank you to Michael Pisarri, my talented and incredible photographer; Mariana Velasquez, my food stylist, a true artist at heart and in my eyes one of the best in her profession. To Luis Corrales, my props stylist and dear friend. Thank you all for having the amazing ability to take my ideas and turn them into beautiful images.

And once again the biggest thank-you goes to the United States of America, for giving me the opportunity to represent my Latin culture, my passion and my ideas each and every day.

INDEX